Keeton '87

THEATRE ARTS
IN THE ELEMENTARY CLASSROOM

Grade Four through Grade Six

Barbara T. Salisbury

ANCHORAGE PRESS, INC.
New Orleans, Louisiana

Theatre Arts in the Elementary Classroom
Grade Four Through Grade Six

ISBN 0-87602-025-2

Graphic Design: Susan Russell

Illustration: Susie Monday

FOREWORD

Barbara T. Salisbury, building on her training and extensive teaching experience, has now created two outstanding theatre arts textbooks for the elementary classroom teacher. My reading of Salisbury's manuscript began in a large metropolitan airport waiting room. In the midst of the *Why, What, How?* chapter, the material came alive as three young children, two girls and one boy, began playing nearby. "This is my house," announced the boy as he ran about checking the seats, completely involved in his play, totally oblivious to the throng of people coming and going. The girls joined him in the house. They pantomimed kitchen utensils and discussed the meal they were preparing.

After a few minutes of play, one of the girls picked up a small stick of wood which she immediately turned into an airplane. The other children joined her on the floor and all three went on an imaginary flight, spontaneously describing the plane and the sights they were seeing. The adults looked on occasionally, always without comment. When the adults called the children to go on their separate ways, their dramatic play ended as abruptly as it had begun.

Obviously these were younger children, unaffected by adult expectations concerning their free dramatic play. By using the theatre arts activities in this text the teacher can guide older students to return to the more uninhibited, spontaneous creativity of their early school years. The older children bring longer attention spans, more maturity, and self control, qualities which enhance all of their drama activities.

Structured around the specific objectives or essential elements to be taught in kindergarten through sixth grade, the two volumes approach the subject of theatre arts in a manner not previously available in textbook form. Expressive use of the body and voice, creative drama, and aesthetic growth through appreciation of theatrical events, serve as the three basic objectives for all grades. The charts on pages 24-25 detail these essential elements and activities by grade level.

At each grade additional objectives and exercises are added to help teachers and students realize the major values and goals of theatre arts, including:

- **helping the children to develop to their fullest potential in** all areas of study

- **helping children realize that the goal in the elementary school is not to put on a play for an audience, but to help them develop their imagination, creativity and appreciation of the art of theatre**

- **learning that theatre arts is a subject in its own right while also being used as an aid to all subjects in the curriculum**

The keys to success in theatre arts activities are clearly presented by Salisbury in very specific terms, such as control, discipline, warm-ups, warm-downs, visualization, questions, organization, etc. Her knowledge of the child's interests and abilities by grade level is clearly demonstrated in her selection of appropriate material and activities. Shadow plays, puppet activities, delightful stories and formal plays are interspersed within the text. All are designed for classroom use. The activities range from those lasting a few minutes to full length sessions of thirty to sixty minutes.

Since many of the drama activities can be successfully repeated at different ages, Salisbury gives a cross-reference guide for easy access to other level activities with information for simplifying or enriching given concepts.

For all age levels, Salisbury, in Chapter Five, correlates drama with other subject areas including language, mathematics, and science. She also gives ideas for the use of drama with special populations from the academically gifted to the economically deprived.

Assessing the students' work in theatre arts is the subject of the last chapter. Here Salisbury offers several options for the evaluation of the various types of theatre activities, including a checklist and rating scale guide. Emphasis is placed on measuring each student against his or her own potential with reference to the individual's progress, rather than comparing them against each other.

This book allows teachers with or without formal training in theatre arts to guide children to achieving their greatest potential in both curricular and extra-curricular theatre arts activities.

In a recent creative drama session with fourth grade students, the shyest, most withdrawn child in the class was found actively participating for the first time. She was clearly concentrating and revealing an imagination not previously noticed by the teacher. During the evaluation period the girl commented: "I was having so much fun, that I forgot to be afraid." Ideally, all teachers will use Salisbury's excellent text in the spirit of learning and sharing as they and the children have rewarding, creative fun. During these creative periods all children will benefit as they develop their concentration, imagination and knowledge of the world.

Equally important are the formal theatre experiences which the students have as audience members. Since students are often more familiar with television and film, Salisbury uses these as a comparison and contrast to theatre. She also notes that theatre for children consists of adults (high school age and up) performing for children, for it is the script and the audience that make theatre for children, not the age of the actors.

To receive maximum educational benefit, the audience members should be prepared before seeing any production. The vicarious experiences of the young audience, through the lives of the characters of the story, be it comic or serious, encourage emotional and aesthetic growth.

After seeing effective productions, many children leave the theatre interested in playing out some of the scenes. They often spontaneously take on the characteristics of the major roles, roaring like a lion or strutting and bragging like the mischievous rogues as they leave the theatre. An analysis and discussion of the theatre experience as well as recreating it in creative drama sessions are important classroom followup activities for audience members.

Salisbury's text is an excellent guide to combining creative fun and serious work so that school children have exciting, memorable learning experiences in theatre arts.

Coleman A. Jennings, Chairman
Department of Drama
The University of Texas at Austin

PREFACE

Theatre Arts in the Elementary Classroom, Grade Four Through Grade Six, is directed to teachers who think they may have limited experience using drama in the classroom. In truth, however, many teachers have used drama more than they know, as a number of teachers who have read this manuscript have discovered. They found the lessons on sensory recall and rhythmic movement, for example, reassuringly familiar — they just didn't know they were "doing drama" before. The same is true for lessons on dialogue, pantomime and others. Consequently, the intent of this book is to familiarize teachers, who may or may not have used theatre arts activities before, with the concepts and methodology of drama and with the importance of drama for children.

The premise of this book, and of its companion volume for teachers of kindergarten through third grade, is that theatre, as one of the fine arts, should be taught in the classroom as a subject in its own right. While theatre arts activities complement many aspects of child growth and development, they do so only because of the integrity of the art form itself. By becoming directly involved in the process of creating drama, children acquire an understanding of theatre arts, as well as an understanding of themselves and the society they live in.

The book is organized to provide very specific and practical help to the teacher.

Chapter One, for example, is both theoretical and practical. It deals with the "nitty gritty" of drama, and it gives tips about classroom management when teaching theatre arts lessons. A scope and sequence chart shows how various dramatic concepts develop sequentially over the years, from kindergarten through sixth grade. (Note: in this chapter, and in succeeding chapters, the term "essential elements" is used. These "essential elements" are terms adopted by the State of Texas Board of Education and I have used them as a means to organize the activities in the book. Other terminology may be used by other states. The important point, however, is not in individual labels, but rather in concepts which are the real building blocks of the art. No matter what you call them, when the elements of drama are combined effectively, they produce theatre that is powerful — theatre, whether formal or informal, which moves people to tears or laughter, theatre which lends insight about what it means to be human.)

Chapters Two through Four are grade level chapters. Each grade has a chapter of its own, so that teachers will have ready access to useful materials. These materials are presented as lesson plans, with concepts, objectives, materials, and procedures clearly stated, and graphically arranged so they can be easily followed. Often, specific questions and comments are written as if the teacher were speaking directly to the students. Such a format seems the clearest and most direct way to demonstrate the progression of each lesson; the comments, however, should not necessarily be followed verbatim. Each teacher will want to adjust and adapt the lessons according to individual styles and the needs of specific classes.

The first lesson for each grade in Chapters Two through Four is called **Getting Started**. This lesson is designed to introduce drama in classes where the children have not previously participated in theatre arts activities. Even those who have experience in drama, however, should find the lesson a good review.

After the introductory lesson, the lessons within each grade level chapter are grouped according to specific drama concepts, such as rhythmic movement, pantomime, sensory awareness, and others. Three or more lessons for each concept are presented, arranged from the simple to the more complex. Rather than teaching all the lessons under one concept before moving on to the next, however, I would encourage teachers to mix and match, for more variety. For example, you may want to start with a rhythmic movement lesson, followed by a sensory awareness lesson or a creative drama lesson.

On the other hand, you may find that a given class needs or wants more work in a certain concept — rhythmic movement, for example. In that case, simply refer to the Cross Reference Guide at the beginning of your grade level chapter. The guide lists page numbers of other lessons dealing with the concept for the grade lower than yours, your grade, and the grade higher. You need not be concerned about teaching lessons more than once — whether repeated during the same year or in successive years. The lessons are open-ended so that each experience can be different. And, just as children enjoy hearing favorite stories over and over again, they will enjoy repeating favorite drama lessons several times.

One of the unique features of the grade level chapters is the way in which the essential element labeled "aesthetic growth through the appreciation of theatrical events" is presented. The lessons are participatory in nature, just as they are for the other essential elements. Lessons in audience etiquette, for example, involve the students in practicing the proper behavior, rather than just talking about it. Lessons on analyzing certain aspects of a play are taught by working with a real script which the students use as a model to enact and analyze. Lessons on the similarities and differences among television, film and live theatre are taught by having the students use real or imagined cameras and viewfinders to demonstrate the differences. The lessons are intended to prepare them so they will be able to appreciate and understand the unique qualities of live theatre.

Chapter Five is different from the other chapters; it deals with using drama as a technique to teach other subjects, and to teach special student populations. Many teachers have found drama to be an effective tool to teach other curricular areas. Ideas relating drama to specific concepts in other subjects are described in this chapter.

For maximum success in using drama as a teaching tool, the children should be quite familiar with the drama process itself. Only then should it be applied to other subjects. Drama is also a powerful tool to use with special children — whether they have physical, mental or emotional handicaps, or whether they are singled out because they are academically gifted. This chapter gives suggestions for ways to use drama with such children.

The final chapter, Chapter Six, deals with assessment. While many people seem discouraged about assessing creative activities, including theatre, assessment is a fact of educational life. The essential elements of theatre can be as effectively assessed as the essential elements in language arts, mathematics or social studies. Initially, the objective stated at the opening of each lesson should provide some help — if the child completes the task, the objective is met. It's that simple. Aspects such as concentration, imagination, non-verbal expression and others are more difficult to assess. This chapter includes a variety of assessment possibilities and tools which teachers can adapt for use in their specific classrooms.

I fervently hope that teachers will find there just aren't enough lessons in this book — that they will want more! Consequently the Appendices included address that desirable dilemma. Appendix A is a list of "Idea Starters," categorized by subject. The activities are briefly described and may be used as presented, or expanded on. Appendix B provides an annotated list of children's literature suitable for dramatization. Appendix C is an annotated bibliography of other resource books about creative drama, puppetry, and drama with special populations. It also includes a brief list of music the teacher may find useful.

Many people have contributed to this book and to its companion volume in very special ways. Countless children, university students and classroom teachers have acted as willing "guinea pigs" as I tried out materials with them. Their feedback has been invaluable, helping me to eliminate unnecessary ideas while focusing on materials that truly work.

Two mentors over the years have influenced my philosophy and direction. One is Geraldine Brain Siks, whose belief that children should be taught *about* drama, *through* drama, led her to distill concepts so they could be taught in the elementary classroom. The other is Agnes Haaga, whose conviction that drama is inside everyone led her to develop a leadership style which brings release, joy, and knowledge about self and humankind to the participants. Together these two have opened doors to the joyful discipline of the art of drama. For that I thank them, as do generations of others.

In addition, several people have given specific encouragement in the development of these particular books. Coleman A. Jennings, chairman of my department, first urged me to write them and was kind enough to write a Foreword. Orlin Corey, my publisher and friend, said, in effect, "Yes, there is a need for such work — let's give it a go." And my husband, J. Robert Wills, not only relinquished the computer, but was my hardest critic — pointing out vagueries, jargon, and leaps of logic. My heartfelt thanks to all.

ACKNOWLEDGEMENTS

"Fog," from *Chicago Poems* by Carl Sandburg. Copyright © 1916 by Holt, Rinehart and Winston, Inc.; renewed 1944 by Carl Sandburg. Reprinted by permission of Harcourt Brace Jovanovich, Inc.

Permission to adapt "The Squire's Bride," from *My Book House*, © The United Educators, Inc.

"Why Mosquitoes Buzz in People's Ears," by Monica Michell, reprinted with her kind permission.

"The Bad Joke That Ended Well," "The Sorcerer's Apprentice," "The Stone in the Road," "The Wise People of Gotham," from *Stories to Dramatize*, by Winifred Ward, reprinted with permission of Anchorage Press, copyright © 1952, renewed, 1980 and 1981.

Permission to adapt "The Wind and Sun," from *The Fables of Aesop*, by Joseph Jacobs, copyright © 1964, Macmillan Co.

Special appreciation to the following:

   Monica Michell for sharing her ideas about using drama in the museum;

   Charlotte Tiencken for sharing her expertise about using drama with children who are culturally different and economically deprived, as well as sharing her ideas for situation role playing;

   The Texas Education Agency for sharing their working documents on the assessment of theatre arts.

CONTENTS

Chapter I:
WHY? WHAT? HOW?

"Well, I got concentration . . . You have to be right on top of things." (Paul, age 9)
"When I came in I didn't know how to express my feelings very well." (Jan, age 10)
"I learned how it is to be another person. (Susan, age 9)
"You can't be all tight inside. You have to relax." (Erik, age 9)
"You pretend like it is real, that it is really happening. Not that you just pretend, but really make other people see that it is really there." (Kim, age 10)

The comments above were made by children in a fifth grade class after they had participated in a series of theatre arts lessons. They were responding to a question about what they had learned. Obviously, they had learned a lot.

This introductory chapter essentially capsulizes the "why, what, and how" issues of teaching theatre arts in the elementary school. The "why" is addressed in the Background section, which describes the nature of theatre and the values its study brings to elementary school children. The "what" issue receives focus in the section on Theatre Elements and Concepts. Each of the three essential elements is described and defined. The "how" issues are discussed in two sections: 1) the Creative Drama Process describes the format used for lessons in this book, which the teacher, in turn, can use to develop other lessons; 2) the Strategies and Management section provides suggestions for setting up a creative environment in which the children and teacher will feel successful. The final section of the chapter returns to the "what" — it is a scope and sequence chart showing the sequential development of concepts from kindergarten through grade six.

WHY STUDY THEATRE ARTS?

The Background

Theatre, or drama, is an integral part of the human experience. One has only to recall one's early childhood days, or watch young children at play, to realize that drama is a natural form of expression. One sees children playing house, cowboys, school, secret agents, characters from television — whoever and whatever captures their imagination. Such dramatic play is one of the most important ways children learn. It is a way to experience the world, to try on different roles, to walk in another's footsteps, to see "What it would be like *if*..."

Just as dramatic play is integral to each individual's experience, it is also integral to the history of the human species. In prehistoric times, aborigines would gather around the fire to act out the day's hunt, or evoke spirits to assist them in a battle, or petition the gods for rain. The Greeks are known not only for the Olympics, but also for their plays. People would spend all day, several days in succession, watching play festivals. Throughout the ages, in every culture, one finds evidence of theatre. Today, we commemorate many kinds of events, from inaugurations to football games, with parades and pageantry. Theatre can be found in almost every community, whether it is done by a group of friends, or a community group, or a professional company. Theatre is one way people have found to grapple with, and reflect upon, the problems and the joys of the world.

Values and Goals

There are two major goals for studying theatre arts:
>   *to help each child develop his or her potential,*
>   *to help each child understand and appreciate the art of theatre.*

Although the two are separated for discussion purposes, the goals of each should constantly reinforce each other.

2

Child Development

Children grow in many ways — physically, mentally, socially, creatively, spiritually. The following remarks suggest ways that participation in the theatre arts help the child grow and develop.

The theatre arts seek to help children develop an awareness of themselves as *physical beings*. The body and the voice comprise the instrument with which one creates and communicates. Self-confidence develops as children begin to recognize and appreciate their own capabilities, and their ability to communicate.

The theatre arts seek to help children become aware of themselves as *creative beings*. During the creative experience, one becomes so involved in the activity that ideas flow in rapid succession, imagination soars, and relationships are perceived. In drama, suddenly the movement, the words, the total expression are truthful and right. Even if the experience is momentary, one feels at once exhilarated and satisfied.

The theatre arts seek to help children envision themselves as *organizers of experience*. They learn to solve problems and to shape and control what is happening, by using their minds and bodies to give form to the art.

The theatre arts seek to help children appreciate themselves as *reflective beings,* responding thoughtfully to people, situations and the environment. Drama encourages attentive listening and observing, as they learn to discuss and analyze their own experiences and those of others.

The theatre arts seek to help children become aware of themselves as *social beings*. Drama takes place within the framework of a group. In order to create with others, children need to develop a sensitivity toward their classmates which allows mutual trust and respect to build, as they participate in the give and take of improvised drama. The content of drama helps them to empathize with and become more understanding of the feelings and actions of others.

The Art of Theatre

The goal is to help the children understand and appreciate the art of drama, which is a story told by means of dialogue and action. There are two levels of understanding involved: an intuitive understanding and an intellectual understanding. Because children come to school fully steeped in play, they have already begun to grasp intuitively the essence of drama. Experience in the theatre arts which is totally involving to the individuals enhances this intuitive understanding. As they mature, children also like to understand intellectually what is happening. Theatre to them is a meaningful game in which knowing more about the rules makes the game more fun to play. This knowledge also gives them more freedom to manipulate and design dramatic structure for themselves.

By studying theatre arts, students learn to:
- *understand character objectives*
- *understand inner and outer characteristics of characters*
- *understand plot structure*
- *understand the function of spectacle, including setting, props, lights, and costumes*
- *work together to create drama*
- *appreciate good literature*
- *appreciate theatrical events*
- *evaluate and make aesthetic judgments*

If a child consistently develops a character, knowing who, what, where and why about the character, if he or she consistently creates plots with beginning, middle, climax, and end, if he or she can either watch or participate in a scene and state its strengths and weakness, both in acting and plot development, one can be reasonably certain the child has an intellectual understanding of theatre.

To summarize, the study of theatre arts is really the study of life. The child learns more about himself or herself, more about other people, through acting out and reflecting upon human experiences.

WHAT IS MEANT BY THEATRE ARTS IN THE ELEMENTARY SCHOOL?

Theatre Elements and Concepts

The focus of studying theatre arts in the elementary grades is not to train actors, but rather to nurture each child's creative and expressive potential as he or she learns about the art of theatre.

There are three broad categories which are called "essential elements," in this book:

1) *Expressive use of the body and voice;*
2) *Creative drama;*
3) *Aesthetic growth through appreciation of theatrical events.*

The first two involve learning by doing, and the third involves learning by receiving and responding.

Essential Element One: Expressive use of the body and voice

Each person uses an "instrument" to communicate and express ideas. This "instrument," quite simply, is limited to one's body and voice. In order to increase expressive skills, the instrument needs to be "tuned" and the player needs to understand the capabilities of the instrument. The following is a brief description of those components, or concepts, which lead to increased expressive skills. The italicized words are concepts for which there are specific activities suggested in Chapters Two, Three, Four.

Movement activities are very important. They serve to free the child's energy and emotions; they allow the child to become aware of the workings of the body and to control them; they increase the ability to communicate; they help to focus the child's imagination. The movement activities in this book are rhythmic and interpretive. *Rhythmic movements* are those which require moving and expressing according to a particular rhythmic pattern. *Interpretive movements* depict non-human roles or abstract concepts, such as fire, wind, power, love.

The body acts and responds because of the senses. *Sensory awareness* activities attempt to sharpen perception and appreciation of how the senses help us to know and enjoy the world. *Sensory recall* activities help the

5

children to remember the way things feel, look, sound, smell and touch, and to recreate those sensations even when they are present only in the imagination, not physically.

Expressive use of the body and voice involves movement, the senses, and feelings. Feelings, or emotions, are the core of being human, and the core of drama. Joy, sadness, fear, melancholy, boredom, contentment only begin a list of emotions that could continue for pages. Children need to recognize and begin to understand their emotions and to realize that feelings are part of what it means to be human. Activities in *emotional recall* help children understand that they are not alone in experiencing certain feelings, and help them empathize with others.

Body movement, the use of the senses, and emotional recall are necessary for pantomime. *Pantomime* is the use of movement and gesture to express ideas and feelings. It is communication through action, not words. Pantomime, sometimes referred to as "body language," is an important building block of speech. It precedes speech in development, but also extends and reinforces speech.

Practice in speaking helps children become fluent in verbal communication, as well as promoting clear articulation and voice control. Children use *original dialogue* as they learn to express themselves by what they say, the words, and how they say it, the voice. Pitch, volume, intensity, rate of speed are all part of vocal communication.

Essential Element Two: Creative Drama

Creative drama is defined by the Children's Theatre Association of America as "an improvisational, non-exhibitional, process-centered form of theatre in which participants are guided by a leader to imagine, enact, and reflect upon human experiences."* Put another way, the teacher helps the children to think, to imagine, to clarify their ideas, so they can act them out, using their own words and movement to express what they want to communicate — not for an audience, but for themselves and their classmates.

The dramatization is based either on a piece of literature, or on an original story developed by the children. The children *improvise* as they act out a situation. That is, they don't plan out exactly what they will say or do before-

6   *"Terminology for Drama/Theatre With and For Children: A Redefinition," *Children's Theatre Review* 28 (Winter 1978): 10-11

hand, but they do have a general idea of the plot and who the characters are.

Characterization involves more than just knowing who the characters are — more, for instance, than knowing that the character is a bank teller, a robber, or a policeman. It involves imagining the *physical attributes* of the character. Is the character big, small, muscular, frail? Does the character move with big, heavy, slow steps? Light, quick, bouncy steps? Is the character wearing a costume that might affect the movement, like a king's robe or an elegant ball gown or a space suit? Characterization also involves knowing what the *objective* of the character is. That is, what does the character want to do — to surprise someone, to hide, to scare, to persuade, to apologize, to tease…? Knowing the objective of a character often helps determine how the character moves. For example, if the objective of a scuba diver is to explore a sunken ship, the diver will move quite differently than if the objective is to rescue a fellow diver from a shark. *Attitude* is another aspect of characterization which affects what the character does and how he or she does it. For example, imagine that the objective is "to hide." If the character is frightened, he or she will show that while trying to find a hiding place. If the character is mischievous, he or she will act quite differently while finding a hiding place. Another aspect of characterization is the way a character *speaks*. For example, in the story of "Hansel and Gretel," how would the witch's voice be different from Gretel's? How might the voice of a bully be different from the voice of someone who is very timid? How something is said reveals as much about a character as the actual words that are spoken.

There are several concepts which will help the children develop original stories, or *plots*. Understanding plot development, of course, is as necessary for composition and appreciation of literature as it is for theatre arts. The analysis of plot *structure* can be very complex, but for the elementary level, it has been limited to "beginning, middle, climax and end." Most plots are centered around a *conflict* of some sort. Specific activities help the children understand the basic causes of conflict — person vs. person, person vs. environment, person vs. self. Where a story takes place, the *setting,* is also important to plot development. The possibilities for action in a supermarket are quite different than they would be in a cave, or on the moon, or at the beach. The *time* of a story can also be important. Time can refer to a time in history —

present day, the Civil War, the year 2086 a.d. — or a time of day, such as three o'clock in the afternoon or three o'clock in the morning. In the latter example, a doorbell ringing in the middle of the night would probably be reacted to in quite a different way than a doorbell in the middle of the afternoon.

All of the concepts on plot development and characterization cannot be taught at once, of course. At the end of this chapter, you will find a scope and sequence chart which will indicate when the various concepts are introduced.

All of the creative drama activities involve improvisation, whether the children are playing the characters or whether they are using *puppets* to play the characters. Children enjoy puppets, and sometimes those children who are inhibited at first, find it easier to participate if they have a puppet to "hide behind." In Chapters Two and Three, there are instructions for making simple hand and shadow puppets. The making of the puppets, however, is only the first step. Bringing them alive through movement and voice is the most important part of using puppets in a theatre arts activity.

In the sixth grade, there are lessons which deal with *"situation role playing."* The activities basically center around situations in which people have differing points of view, or react differently from one another. The lessons try to help the children develop understanding and respect for various viewpoints, and also to be considerate of other people's feelings.

Essential Element Three: Aesthetic growth through appreciation of theatrical events

Theatre exists when there are four very basic components present:
1) an *idea,* story, or play, which involves action;
2) those presenting the action, the *actors;*
3) a *space* to act in, be it classroom, stage, basement, or backyard;
4) those watching the action, the *audience.*

The term "audience," has a different connotation within the educational theatre context. When doing drama in the classroom, occasionally some children will watch, while others act out an idea or a scene. Those watching are the "audience." Children in the elementary school are *not* required, nor encouraged, to perform a formal play for the entertainment of an audience. They are encouraged to see as many live theatre performances as possible.

Just as children become better appreciators of art by seeing great works of art, so children must see plays, preferably in a theatre, to fully understand the art of theatre. Theatre arts concepts are reinforced as the children see the actors use their bodies and voices to create characters, much like the work the children have been doing in their own class. There is an excitement, a sense of "magic" that occurs in the theatre, when the actors are right there with the audience, that is quite different from watching television or going to a movie.

Theatre conventions

There are certain theatre conventions which adults take for granted. Students, however, should know about them before attending a theatrical event. For instance, before the performance the lights inthe lobby may blink off and on to tell the audience to take their seats because the performance will soon begin. Then when the lights dim in the theatre and go out, the performance is about to begin. If a curtain is used inthe performance, when it goes up, or opens, the performance has begun. (The curtain going down, or closing, indicates the end of an act or the end of the performance.) Sometimes, at the end of a scene or an act, all the lights will be turned off — a moment called a "blackout." After a performance is over, the actors come back on stage, in bright light, to take their bows while the audience applauds — called a "curtain call." Then the house lights come on and people leave.

Audience etiquette

When students know what to expect, they usually know how to behave. There is a specific lesson in Chapter Two dealing with audience etiquette. It is a good lesson for each grade to review before attending a performance. Proper behavior in the theatre is necessary for two reasons. Most obvious is the fact that one should be considerate of other members of the audience who want to see and hear what is happening on stage. Less obvious may be the actors' relationship with the audience, which is what separates live theatre from film and television. The theatre experience is complete only when there is an audience. The audience members actually help the actors when they listen attentively, laugh at appropriate times, or even gasp when something unexpected happens. Generally, the better and more attentive the audience, the better the performance.

Similarities and differences in television, film, and live theatre

Drama was defined earlier as a story told by means of dialogue and action. That definition is accurate for film and television, as well as live theatre. In fact, the concepts described before with regard to the expressive use of body and voice, and creative drama are true for film and television, too. There are, however, a number of differences.

The most apparent difference, of course, is the actual presence of actors in a live theatre performance. Besides the special relationship between the actors and the audience, there are other differences, such as the setting, the acting, the time of action, special effects, camera angles, and the position of the audience. While there are specific lessons dealing with those differences in the following chapters, a brief overview follows here.

Because the camera is so mobile, the *setting* of the stories can be shown realistically and in great detail in films and television. (The word "film" will be used here to refer to both movies and television. References to "theatre" will refer to live theatre, rather than movie theatres.) In the theatre, the setting is limited to what can be represented on the stage, by sets, set pieces (such as furniture), and lighting. Furthermore, on stage the set pieces must be placed so that the actors can move around easily and so that the audience can see their faces at all times; whereas for film, cameras can move around the furniture to photograph the actors wherever they may be. Lighting on stage can indicate the approximate time of day, but for film, scenes can be shot showing the exact time of day, weather and other environmental conditions. In the theatre, audience members are required to use their imaginations to create the reality of the setting in their minds, based on the "clues" given by the sets and lights.

The *time* the action takes place can also be shown more realistically in films. For example, an actual winter snowstorm can be filmed, but only referred to or indicated on the stage. "Flashbacks," or scenes that are remembered by certain characters, can be shown immediately and realistically on film. In the theatre, flashbacks are possible, but may be more difficult for the audience to follow. Because the camera not only can move, but can start and stop, the illusion of time passing can be realistically portrayed. For example, a character may be fixing breakfast in a bathrobe in one scene, and, in less than an instant, the film can show her walking down the street with briefcase in hand. In the theatre, the costume and set changes would take actual performance time. With film, the actors can change clothes, adjust makeup and go to a different location before the camera starts rolling again. The film audience is not consciously aware of all the adjustments that have to be made. They simply accept the "fact" that the time of the story has changed.

There are some differences in *acting* for the theatre and for films, too. The basic difference has to do with the "size" of the action. Because the camera can move so close to the actor, a mere twitch of the eyebrow can be filmed and the audience will see it. Such a twitch would be lost in the theatre, because the audience is too far away to see such subtle action. Gestures and movements must be very realistic for film, or the character will not seem believable. Depending on the size of the theatre and the position of the audience, the stage actor chooses gestures carefully so they can be seen by all. The gestures must seem realistic to the audience, but if they were seen closely, they might be somewhat exaggerated. The stage actor must also move so that the audience can see at least part of his or her face most of the time. Rarely, for instance, would the actor stand with the back to the audience while talking to another character. The voice is used differently, too, depending upon whether one is acting for the stage or film. A character can whisper on film and the audience will understand every word, because the microphone is very close. On stage, such a whisper would be inaudible; the actor would have to use a "stage whisper," which is quite loud and includes exaggerating the consonants. The stage actor learns how to project his or her voice, so that it can be heard in the very back row and yet not seem to be shouting. The film actor, however, can and must speak in a normal voice.

Special effects are used for both theatre and film, but there are limitations to special effects in theatre — most of which have to do with danger, and the illusions which can be created with the camera. One readily accepts car chases, crashes, fires and fights as being "true" on film, because they appear so realistic. What the film audience doesn't see, of course, is all the very detailed planning that goes on to create these effects; nor do they see the special safety suits and the ring of people standing by to extinguish a fire, for example, immediately after the stunt. The audience isn't aware that the camera stops after the stunt and then starts again, usually on a different scene. Nor is the audience aware that the battleship they see in a film, may, in fact, be merely a twenty inch replica floating in a tub with a wave making machine. Obviously these kinds of effects are not possible in the theatre. Certainly there are special effects possible in the theatre, such as fog, explosions, storms, and many others, but the reality of stage effects depends a lot on the willingness of the audience to accept the illusion and imagine the details.

The eye of the camera really becomes the eye of the film audience. *Camera angles* allow the audience to see minute details and various points of view. One can see, for example, a character at a distance walking down the street, and then see the character in a close-up in which only the face fills the entire screen. The camera "chooses" what the audience will see, whether it is a crowd, two people, one person, or only hands gesturing.

The *position of the audience* is related to camera angles, with regard to films. The audience can "move around," because the camera moves around, even though the audience is seated in one place during the whole time. In the theatre, such seeming movement is not possible. The actors move, the audience doesn't. There are a number of audience seating arrangements in theatres. Sometimes the stage is in the middle, with the audience all around. Sometimes, the audience is seated on three sides of the stage. Sometimes, and most commonly, the audience is seated in front of the stage. In the latter, it seems as if the audience is looking through the fourth wall of whatever setting is on stage.

On an audience commitment continuum, television requires the least amount of commitment, because the viewer can switch channels at will. Some viewers even keep track of two programs at once, by switching channels frequently. It is possible to walk around, eat, stretch, and so on during the program. Films in movie theatres require more audience commitment. The viewer physically goes to the movie theatre and pays money to see the film. Talking during the film, while inconsiderate of the rest of the audience, will not affect the performances of the actors. In most cases, television and film dramas require very little imagination from the audience, because everything is presented so realistically. Live theatre requires the greatest amount of audience commitment. Not only does the audience physically go to the theatre and pay money to see the performance, but they are necessary participants in the performance. The theatre audience says, in effect, "Yes, I'm willing to believe the people are in front of a fireplace," even though it is obvious that they are looking at lights and cellophane flames. The theatre audience uses imagination and concentration to help the actors create the play. They respond, not by talking, but by laughing and applauding at appropriate times. The actors know the audience is there. Together, they create the theatre experience. Together, they create the magic of belief.

Aesthetic judgments

By participating in theatre art activities and attending live theatre performances, students learn how to evaluate and make informed aesthetic judgments. In other words, they learn to tell *why* they liked a particular play or performance, or why they did not like it. They learn how to analyze the behavior of various characters. They learn how to analyze plot, recognize conflicts, predict resolutions and make suggestions for alternative courses of action.

Obviously, different schools will attend different performances, and performances will vary from year to year. In order to provide a concrete model to analyze and evaluate, a play script has been included in this book, for each grade. The students can act out the play as simply or elaborately as they wish, or they can just read the play outloud and discuss it according to the lesson. The model can then be applied to whatever performances are attended. The focus for analysis in each grade is tied into the character and plot concepts they have been learning about in the first two essential elements. For example, in Chapter Two, the students are learning about the physical attributes of characterization and character objectives. When they analyze characters after seeing a play, they will focus on those same concepts.

Chapters Two, Three, Four deal with the three essential elements by category, but there is some overlap. For example, there are lessons on pantomime under both "Expressive use of the body and voice," and "Creative drama." In working with the lessons, teachers will probably begin to pick and choose various activities which can be combined effectively for a particular class. The following discussion of the creative drama process is intended to help teachers plan their own lessons, in addition to using those in the book.

CREATIVE DRAMA PROCESS

The creative drama lessons in Chapters Two, Three, and Four of this book follow a simple format, which is known as the creative drama process. Each lesson is divided into five parts: the introduction, the presentation, the plan for action, the action, and the evaluation. The function of each part is briefly described below. The application of the process is described in detail in the creative drama lessons themselves.

I. Introduction

The introduction provides the motivation for the material which is used as the basis for dramatization. The purpose is to engage the attention of the students and to help them to relate their own experiences to the material. Sometimes this is accomplished by asking the students questions about their own experiences, sometimes by combining discussion with action of some sort which will help them identify with the material.

II. Presentation

If the material for dramatization is a story, it is best presented by telling, not reading. Telling a story allows for eye contact with the students, and makes the story seem more real to them. Before telling the story, or poem, the teacher might want to ask them to listen for something particular. For example, "While you listen to this story, see if you can tell which character felt just as afraid as you have before." Or, "Listen to see how Juan solved his probelm."

If the dramatization is based on students' original stories, the Introduction usually flows right into the Plan for Action, which follows.

III. Plan for Action

A. Plan based on a story or poem.

After the story, the teacher and students make a plan for acting out a portion of the story. The teacher asks questions. The questions may focus on just one character — Pandora in "Pandora's Box," for instance. Depending on the objective of the lesson, questions may refer to such concepts as the attitude of the character or how the character talks. There should always be questions about how the character feels in a certain situation. For example, "How did Pandora feel after she opened the box? How would *you* have felt?" Feelings connect people to other people, causing empathy, whether the people are fictional or real.

Sometimes there are fights or physical conflicts in the story which teachers are understandably leary about acting out. One constant rule is "No Touching!" This rule presents an intriguing challenge to students when there is a scene with obvious physical contact. A few questions from the teacher will help. For example, "How can we make it seem as if the Evils are attacking Pandora without actually touching her?" Ask a couple of students to demonstrate their ideas.

The teacher often decides beforehand how many students will act at any given time. Usually all the students want to play the main characters, so it is a good idea to set up a situation where they can all have that experience. Perhaps all the students can try out a particular character simultaneously, or half the class can play at one time. For example, all could play Pandora just before and after she opens the box. As Pandora, they can all react to imaginary Evils that fly out of the box. Then, later, the roles may be divided among the students for the playing of a scene or the whole story.

The teacher also needs to decide what he or she will do during the playing. There are three possibilities. One is to *"sidecoach."* That is, the teacher gives suggestions from the side, while the students pantomime. They listen and respond appropriately without stopping their action. (There are many sidecoaching suggestions in the creative drama lessons in this book.) A second possibility is to *play a role,* to help the students keep the action going. For example, the teacher could play the "head witch," or a companion to the main character. Always choose a role that has built-in authority to it, so questions can be asked which spur their action while they play. Needless to say, students love it when the teacher plays, too. (Examples of this kind of guidance are given in the lessons.) The third possibility is to stand on the side and simply be an *appreciative audience.*

B. Plan based on original ideas

Sometimes, the students will be working in groups to develop their own scenes. On these occasions, the teacher goes around to each group to help them, if necessary. They need to decide *who* they are, *where* they are, and *what* they are doing. They also need to decide how the scene begins and how it will end. (Specific directions are given in the lessons.) After they have their ideas, they should try playing the scene.

Sometimes, the whole class will be working on one idea. For example, they are all deep sea divers. The teacher asks questions to help them visualize the scene and the action: Why are you making this particular dive? What might you find? What dangers must you be aware of? What equipment do you need? How will you communicate with your diving partner? In this particular situation, the teacher might choose to be the captain of the diving boat who gives them instructions, signals them about approaching danger, tells them when to return to the boat, and so on.

IV. Action

After planning, the students are ready for action. They should all get into their places and be very quiet. When they are quiet, the teacher gives the signal to begin. "Curtain" is a word used by many to signal the beginning and ending of the action.

V. Evaluation

The evaluation is an important part of the process. The children will want to talk about the experience and, furthermore, it gives the teacher a chance to reinforce the objective of the lesson. For example, if the objective was to pantomime very clearly, the following question might be asked: "How could you tell that this diver found a very heavy treasure chest?" Or, "What did Pandora do that let you know she was curious?" The students may also have suggestions about how they could make the scene better. Questions to that effect are appropriate. For example, "How could we improve the scene between the shark and the divers, to make it seem more exciting?"

VI. Plan and Replay

Repeat the process, focusing on another character, or another part of the story, or replaying the first scene to strengthen it. This cycle can be repeated as many times as the teacher and class wish.

Each lesson ends with a brief discussion and reinforcement of the objective.

STRATEGIES AND MANAGEMENT

The key to success in theatre arts activities lies in two areas: *concentration* and *imagination*. The extent to which students concentrate and imagine determines the effectiveness of a particular activity. In many ways, the two are intertwined. Using the imagination involves getting an image, or picture, in one's mind. In order to get that picture, one needs to concentrate, to focus on a particular idea. That kind of focus is necessary, or the student will not know what to do. His or her actions will be vague and may also be disruptive to the rest of the group. Fortunately, there are strategies and management considerations which can greatly assist in achieving success. Topics to be considered in this chapter include selection of material, space, time, atmosphere, warm-ups, control, visualization, questions, grouping, warm-downs, and sharing with an audience.

Selection of material

The lessons in this book have proven to be effective with many classes. However, you, the classroom teacher, know your students best. And if you don't think a particular lesson would interest your class — don't use it! There is a wealth of material to draw from, and almost any lesson can be successfully adapted to different materials.

If the lessons written for your grade seem either too simple or too advanced for your particular class, feel free to use lessons from other grades. Repetition is no problem. In fact, look at the kinds of characters and games children play on their own — they enjoy playing the same thing over and over! Furthermore, in drama, they continue to learn each time they play something.

Space

Some activities can be done without any changes in the usual classroom arrangement. However, some may require more space for the students to work. It may be that you can move furniture to one side to create an open space. Or, perhaps, there is a different room in your building which you can use. Sometimes lunchroom tables and chairs can be moved aside. Or there may be a stage, or a multi-purpose room. One of the hardest spaces to work in is the gymnasium. First, the acoustics are usually such that it is difficult to talk and to hear; second, it is a place where the children are accustomed to making a lot of noise, so discipline can be a problem; third, it is usually too big and the students find it difficult to stay within certain boundaries which are necessary for communication and control.

Time

Your concern with time involves the length of a single drama lesson, and the time of day you do it. There is no set length — some activities may take ten minutes, some may take thirty minutes, or even longer. You may want to combine some of the shorter activities. For example, you could use one rhythmic movement activity and one sensory awareness activity during the same session.

The time of day in which creative drama happens is more important. Students need to be alert and concentrating in order to do creative work. Lessons that are done when students are tired and irritable will only be frustrating to them and to you. Or, if they are already "higher than kites," you will have a difficult time helping them concentrate. (A movement activity in that instance, however, might help release energy and provide focus. See the description of "warm-ups," in this chapter.) The point is to choose a time when the students are most apt to produce creative and concentrated work.

Atmosphere

The atmosphere in the classroom needs to be very supportive and encouraging for the students. You are trying to bring out their most imaginative and creative ideas. They need to trust you and their classmates to be receptive to their ideas. In fact, there are really no "right" or "wrong" answers to questions — as long as they are thoughtful and honestly intended. If you find that some students give "silly" answers, they are either not concentrating or they are trying to get attention, and you need to deal with that either by asking them to rethink their response, or ignoring them. A warning must be added here however: What may seem "silly" to you, may not seem so to the student at all. When you respond seriously, respecting what they have to offer, the students will soon learn to produce their best. You will also find the students modeling your behavior — appreciating what others do and the fact that each person has unique things to offer. "Put-downs" and sarcastic remarks from the students are unacceptable in a creative climate. Drama can be a big confidence builder, and frequently students who have trouble in other subjects will feel better about themselves when they participate in drama.

Warm-ups

Recognizing that elementary students have an abundance of energy, you may want to begin each drama session with a warm-up. A warm-up is usually a movement activity that releases their energy, works their imagination, and prepares them to concentrate. The rhythmic movement and interpretive movement activities in this book, can be used as warm-ups. (Remember, repetition is perfectly fine.)

Control

Each person has his or her own tolerance level for noise. There will be some noise during drama activities — during the planning and acting stages, especially. However, there is a difference between acceptable and unacceptable noise. Acceptable noise is when the students are really involved in the task at hand and ideas are flowing rapidly. Unacceptable noise is when they are "goofing off." Even acceptable noise may rise beyond your tolerance limits and the students will need to be reminded to lower the decibels.

A "control instrument" can be enormously effective for getting the students' attention. A drum, a tambourine, a cymbal, a triangle are all possibilities — better than using your voice to shout above their noise. The students will quickly learn to "freeze" when you strike the instrument, ready to listen for directions. The first lesson for each grade, called *Getting Started,* suggests introducing such a control device. The important thing is to use it consistently, and insist that they respond to it before continuing.

The role you play can also help with control, as was suggested earlier in the discussion about planning the action. For example, if you play the "head witch," in an appropriate scene, you can order the students around and even

20

speak crossly. Because you do it in character, the students will respond appropriately.

Visualization

Never let the students act unless they have a clear idea of what they are going to do, or you will invite confusion and chaos. One technique is to ask them to close their eyes and imagine themselves going through a particular action — you may even want to sidecoach while their eyes are closed. Sometimes the lessons suggest the use of music. If so, play the music and ask them to imagine the action while it is playing. Another technique is to ask them to raise a finger when they have a clear idea of what they plan to do, or to sit down, or give some other observable signal.

Questions

The questioning techique may be the most important consideration of all. The right question at the right time will yield the most thoughtful responses from the students. Questions which are probing generally begin with "why," "how," "where," "what," and "when." These are in contrast to superficial questions which elicit "yes" or "no" responses. The rule of thumb is never to ask a question which might elicit a "no" response, when you *want* to hear a "yes" response. For example, "Do you want to act out the deep sea divers?" You can rest assured that someone will say "No," whether it is meant or not!

Grouping

Students need to learn how to work in groups and how to share with one another. Working in a group is a skill that develops gradually. It is usually best to begin by dividing them into pairs, and then working up to groups of three, four and even five.

They also need to learn to work with classmates who are not their "best friends." There are numerous ways of dividing them into working groups. One, of course, is to count off, with all the "one's" working together, the "two's," and so on. Another is to group them by the first letter of their names — all those whose names begin with A, B or C work together. Or group them by shirt colors, or by seat positions, or by those who have a younger brother, an older sister. The possibilities are vast.

Warm-downs

If and when you find the students highly excited after a drama lesson, use a "warm-down" activity to help them relax and prepare them for the next classroom activity. You might play some relaxing music and have them sit down, or lie down and "dream" to the music. You might have them imagine they are melting ice cream cones, or water evaporating, or a cloud moving slowly in the sky, or a raindrop sinking into the earth, or a puppet with no one holding the strings, or a cat sleeping in the sun. The students may even come up with some relaxing images themselves, if you ask.

Sharing with an audience

After students have had many experiences creating drama, some or all of them may wish to share a particular activity with groups outside their own classroom. They may want to share with another class on their own grade level, or older students may want to share with a younger class. When a class has particularly enjoyed dramatizing a certain story — either from a piece of literature or from an original idea — they may want to refine it and strengthen it by rehearsing many times. They may want to videotape rehearsals, so they can see themselves and evaluate what they are doing. Knowing they are going to perform for an audience often provides great incentive to concentrate and prepare thoroughly.

While it is possible for children to use a prepared script, usually the characterization and action turn out to be very stilted and non-creative at the elementary age. If they do work from a script, the script should be approached much like a story is approached. In other words, the script can be read once or twice, the characters discussed, and then portions of the plot can be improvised by the children, before they put the whole thing together. They use their own words, rather than strictly adhering to the script. The script provides the plot structure, just as a story does.

The project can be as simple or elaborate as the teacher and class wish. The entire class may want to be involved in the project in some way. Some might want to gather props together, some may want to experiment with simple lighting, some may want to create simple costumes, some may want to work on sound effects. Such preparations are excellent for building group cooperation skills.

SCOPE AND SEQUENCE

The following pages show the scope and sequence of the concepts as they develop from kindergarten through grade six. Although this volume deals only with grades four through six, teachers may wish to see how the concepts have progressed from the primary grades. The arrows on the chart indicate that a particular concept is continued in the next grade.

THEATRE ARTS
Scope and Sequence — Elementary Grades

Essential Elements	Kindergarten	Grade One	Grade Two	Grade Three
Expressive use of the body and voice	Develop body awareness and spatial perception using · *rhythmic movement* · *imitative movement* Imitate sounds	· *sensory awareness*	· *pantomime* Imitate dialogue	· *sensory recall* · *emotional recall*
Creative drama	Dramatize limited-action stories and poems using · *simple pantomime* · *puppetry*	Dramatize literary selections using · *pantomime* · *shadow play* · *imitative dialogue*		
Aesthetic growth through appreciation of theatrical events				View theatrical events emphasizing · *player-audience relationship* · *audience etiquette*

THEATRE ARTS
Scope and Sequence — Elementary Grades

Grade Four	Grade Five	Grade Six
Develop body awareness and spatial perception using · *rhythmic movement* ———— · *interpretive movement* ———— · *sensory awareness and recall* ———— · *pantomime* ———— · *emotional recall*	· *emotional recall in character* ————	————▸ ————▸ ————▸ ————▸ ————▸ ————▸
Create original dialogue ————		————▸

Dramatize literary selections using
· *pantomime* ————
· *improvisation emphasizing plot structure*
· *characterization emphasizing*
  · *physical attributes*
  · *character objective*
· *original dialogue* ————
· *puppetry* ————
· *shadow play*
	Dramatize original stories using ————
	· *improvisation emphasizing three kinds of conflict*
	· *characterization emphasizing attitude revealed in behavior*
		————▸
		————▸
		· *improvisation emphasizing*
		  · *setting*
		  · *time*
		· *characterization emphasizing speech revealing character* ————▸
		
		· *situation role playing*

View theatrical events emphasizing ———— · *player-audience relationship* · *audience etiquette* · *analysis of physical attributes and objectives of characters* · *recognition of dramatic conflicts* · *prediction of plot resolution*	· *analysis of character's attitude revealed in behavior* · *recognition of kind of conflict* ———— · *prediction of plot resolutions* ———— · *evaluation and aesthetic judgments* ————	————▸ · *analysis of how speech reveals character* ————▸ ————▸ · *suggestions for alternative courses of action*
Recognize similarities and differences among television, film and live theatre emphasizing ———— · *setting* · *acting*	· *time of action* · *special effects*	————▸ · *camera angles* · *position of audience*

25

CONCLUSION

This chapter has tried to explain some of the "bare bones" of what is meant by theatre arts in the elementary classroom: why such study is valuable, what it is about, and how it can be taught effectively. The next step, of course, is to go directly to the chapter which deals with a particular grade level. Actually working with the activities should help clarify and reinforce the basic ideas which were presented in this chapter.

Chapter II:
GRADE FOUR

Fourth graders who have been participating in the theatre arts curriculum, have had experiences in *rhythmic movement,* imitative movement, *sensory awareness, emotional recall, pantomime* and imitative dialogue. Those expressive skills are applied are reinforced in the fourth grade. Instead of imitative movement, however, most students will now be ready for the move abstract concept of *interpretive movement.* And, instead of imitiative dialogue, the students will be creating *original dialogue.*

In creative drama, in addition to using pantomime and puppetry, children will use *improvisation* to learn about *plot structure,* and they will begin to learn about *characterization,* by focusing on the *physical attributes* and the *objective* of a character.

Lessons are included which will assist in the children's aesthetic growth. When they *view a theatre performance* they will have the opportunity to demonstrate their understanding of *audience etiquette* and the *player-audience relationship.* They will also learn how to observe some of the concepts they worked on in the creative drama lessons, such as the *physical attributes* and *objectives of characters* in a play. Their creative drama experiences will also help them recognize *dramatic conflicts.* A play script is included as a *model for analysis.*

The fourth grade lessons also include activities which will help the children recognize *similarities and differences among television, film, and live theatre,* with particular emphasis on the *setting* and the *acting.*

In the event that a class has not had prior experience in classroom drama, the Cross Reference Guide included here provides a ready access to concepts and page numbers. Classes may benefit from activities described in the third grade before they work on the activities for the fourth grade. In any case, the teacher may wish to review earlier lessons. (The third grade activities are in Volume One.)

On the other hand, a given class may demonstrate considerable skill in a certain concept and benefit from deepening their understanding by participating in activities from Grade Five. Children enjoy repeating theatre arts activities, so "borrowing" from another grade level is perfectly acceptable. Repeating activities within the grade level is also acceptable, and, in fact, desirable, because students become more proficient with repetition.

THEATRE ARTS
Cross Reference Guide

Essential Elements	Grade Three Vol. 1	Pg. No.	Grade Four	Pg. No.	Grade Five	Pg. No.
Expressive use of the body and voice	Develop body awareness and spatial perception using · *rhythmic movement* · *imitative movement* · *sensory awareness and recall* · *pantomime* · *emotional recall*	Vol. I: 137-139 139-141 142-145 146-148 149-151	Develop body awareness and spatial perception using · *rhythmic movement* · *interpretive movement* · *sensory awareness and recall* · *pantomime* · emotional recall	 35-36 37-39 40-43 45-46 47-48	· *rhythmic movement* · *interpretive movement* · *sensory awareness and recall* · *pantomime* · *emotional recall in character*	112-113 114-117 118-121 122-123 124-125
	Imitate dialogue	152-153	Create original dialogue	49-50	Original dialogue	126-128

Creative drama	Dramatize literary selections using
	· *pantomime*
	· *shadow play*
		154-170
		171-182
			Dramatize literary selections using
			· pantomime
			· improvisation emphasizing plot structure
			· characterization emphasizing
			  · physical attribute
			  · character objectives
			  · original dialogue
			· original dialogue
			· shadow play
			· puppetry
				
				51-56
				
				57-61
				
				62-65
				66-70
				
				71-74
				75-80
				81-84
					Dramatize original stories using
					· *pantomime*
					· *improvisation and original dialogue emphasizing three kinds of conflict*
					· *characterization emphasizing attitude revealed in behavior*
					· *puppetry*
						129-130
						
						131-136
						
						137-140
						141-143

Aesthetic growth through appreciation of theatrical events	View theatrical events emphasizing: · *player-audience relationship* · *audience etiquette*	183-184 185-186	View theatrical events emphasizing: · player-audience relationship · audience etiquette · analysis of physical attributes and objectives of characters · recognition of dramatic conflicts · prediction of plot resolution Recognize similarities and differences among television, film, and live theatre emphasizing: · *setting* · *acting*	85-86; 102-103 87 88-102 104-105	· *analysis of character's attitude revealed in behavior* · *recognition of kind of conflict* · *prediction of plot resolutions* · *evaluation and aesthetic judgements* · *time of action* · *special effects*	144-154 154-156 157-158

' 31

A NOTE BEFORE BEGINNING: The sentences which are in italic are stated as if the teacher is talking directly to the children. They are either directions, questions, or sidecoaching comments. Sidecoaching means that you are observing the children and making comments while they are acting, in order to spark their imaginations, suggest new ideas, or encourage their good work.

The italicized sentences are only intended as suggestions. Each teacher has an individual style, and should tailor remarks and questions to that style, as well as to the needs of the particular class.

GETTING STARTED

Objective: To develop an initial understanding of drama, through discussion and action

Materials: A control device, such as a drum, or tambourine

Write the word "drama" on the board, scrambling the letters. For example,
> *ramad*

Tell the class that the word is the name of something they are going to be doing in class. They need tools to do it and they have all of the tools they need with them right now. See if they can unscramble the letters.

What tools are needed to do drama? Accept all answers, but the basic tools to emphasize are

> *the voice,*
> *the body,*
> *the mind.*

Each tool is very important. Ask why they think the mind is important. Stress the importance of *imagination*.

Tell the students that today they are going to exercise their imaginations:

> *Find your own place in space, where you can work without bumping into anyone else.*
> *At your feet you will see an imaginary length of rope.*

When I give the signal to start, you are to pick up the rope and begin to use it in some way. Think of as many things to do with the rope as you can.

Use the drum or the tambourine to give the signal to begin.

After two minutes, give the same signal to stop.

How many thought of over five things to do with the rope?

Find out some of their ideas by having volunteers demonstrate one idea each.

Discuss imagination:

Why is imagination important in drama?

How is it important in almost all of life?

Why would a scientist who is trying to find a cure for cancer need to use imagination?

ESSENTIAL ELEMENT ONE:
EXPRESSIVE USE OF BODY AND VOICE

Concept: Develop body awareness and spatial perception through *rhythmic movement*

HEAVY AND LIGHT

Objective: To create the illusion of being very heavy and very light

Materials: A drum or tambourine to accompany the movement

Tell the class to imagine they are jogging around the playground, only they are to do it in place. Direct attention to how they use their arms when they jog. Sidecoach:

> *Continue jogging, but imagine you have lead weights on your feet and legs. It is very difficult to move.*
>
> *Now you have weights on your arms, as well.*
>
> *Now there is one around your waist. Feel the weight as you continue to jog.*
>
> *Suddenly the weight around your waist is removed.*
>
> *Next the weights on your arms are gone.*
>
> *Then the weights on your legs and feet are gone.*
>
> *Not only are the weights gone, but somehow you are now only a fraction of your normal weight — almost feather light.*
>
> *You almost bound in the air, you are so light.*
>
> *Float down to the ground, and relax.*

Discuss the feelings of being heavy and light. This activity, incidently, is a good one to use when the chldren are tense and need to relax.

EYES AHEAD

Objective: To observe and follow a rhythmic pattern

Divide the class into groups of five or six. Each group makes a line, so that each person sees only the back of the person directly in front of him or her at all times. The first person in each row is the leader. The leader does a movement for the group to follow that involves *moving only the arms and hands*. The leader should move slowly so others can follow. After a few moments, give a signal to stop.

The first person goes to the back of the line and the second person becomes the leader. This time the leader uses *hands, arms, feet and legs, but does not move forward*.

Each time there is a new leader, give different directions:

Use your whole body, but move in slow motion.
Use your whole body and move forward, being sure your line doesn't interfere with any other line.
Move from side to side.
Stay in place, but move up and down.

FALLING SAFELY

Objective: To fall down safely

Children love to fall down. Frequently when they act out stories, one of them will incorporate falling. This step-by-step sequence will help them to fall safely. Direct them to practice it slowly, several times, while you call out the sequence.

Sequence:
1. *Bend knees slightly*
2. *Bend knees more*
3. *Kneel*
4. *Slide on to one hip*
5. *Put elbow and forearm on the floor*
6. *Put shoulder on the floor*
7. *Put head on floor.*

After they become proficient, add variations, such as the following:

fall in slow motion;
fall in doubletime;
fall as if being hit in the stomach;
trip over an imaginary object.

Students will have other suggestions to add.

Concept: Develop body awareness and spatial perception through *interpretive movement*

SHAKE IT UP!

Objective: To use movement to stimulate the imagination

Ask the students what their bodies do when they are very, very cold. It shivers and shakes. That is what they will do today — shake.

Begin by shaking your hands.
How many different places can you shake them?
   in front
   behind
   overhead
   one high, one low
Add another part of your body.
Add more parts until you are shaking all over.
Shake as fast as you can.
While you are shaking, think of something you have seen that shakes.
   For instance, a cement drill, clothes dryer, cold dog, gelatin, old
   person.
Become the shaking thing you have seen in your imagination.
Now shake slowly. Are you still the same thing or something
   different?
Shake slowly down to the floor. Gradually stop shaking. Relax.
The class might want to mention some of the "shaking" things they became.

BIG BEACH BALL

Objective: To totally relax, using the image of a beach ball

*Imagine that you are a big, round, beach ball, being bounced back
and forth. You sail through the air and bounce very gently when
you land.*
Bounce back and forth several times.
Suddenly you realize you are losing air.
Gradually slow down until finally you can't bounce any more.
You become flatter and flatter, until all of the air is gone.
Relax.

POWER

Objective: To use movement to interpret the power of a weed

Materials: A cymbal may be used to help build to the climax. Or you
may choose to use a piece of slow, heavy music to help
establish rhythm and mood. Examples are "Mars," from
The Planets Suite, by Holst, or "Gnomes," from *Pictures
at an Exhibition,* by Moussorgsky.

How many of you have gardens at home?
*One of the problems in keeping a garden or lawn looking its best is to
keep it free from weeds.*
What do weeds do to the plants in a garden?
Direct them to get into the smallest position possible. When you give the
signal, they are to grow slowly into a huge, powerful weed. When they are
fully grown they feel so powerful, they feel as if they own the world.
After they have grown, sidecoach:
You see a little plant close to you who dares to get in your way.

You want to get rid of him.
You grow even larger and use your power to crush him and force him out.
You see more plants around you. One by one you eliminate them.
Now you feel as if you are the ruler of the world.

Afterward, discuss when they felt most powerful, and what other feelings they may have had.

How do you think the little plants felt?
What did they do to try to survive?

Direct them to get into the smallest position possible, again. This time they are going to grow into the little plant. Each should think of what kind of plant or shrub to be.

Again, after they have grown, sidecoach:

You feel the sunshine on you and it feels so good.
Suddenly a shadow looms over you.
It is a huge weed closing in on you and trying to crush you.
You try to fight back, but you can't.
You become weaker and weaker.
Finally, you collapse.

Afterward, discuss the feelings of the little plant.

Are there any similar situations among people in real life? You may want to discuss different kinds of power — power which is destructive and power which is constructive — and the different means used with each.

Concept: Develop body awareness and spatial perception through
sensory awareness and sensory recall

LISTEN AND IMAGINE

Objective: To listen to sounds and choose one as the basis for a story

---

Tell the students to close their eyes and listen to the sounds they hear *outside* the classroom. Each person should focus on one of the sounds and listen closely to it.

> *Who might be making the sound? Why?*
> *Is the person doing something or going somewhere?*
> *Think up a little story about the sound.*

After a couple of minutes, tell them to open their eyes and share their story with the person sitting next to them.

FEET REMEMBER

Objective: To use the senses to recall walking on a variety
of surfaces.

This activity is best done with shoes removed. Ask them what their favorite thing is to walk on when they are barefoot. Choose one of the suggestions given, such as grass or sand or mud, and ask them to get up and see if their feet can remember how it feels. After a moment of walking in place, ask them to describe how it feels on their feet.

Then give them other surfaces to recall with their feet. Examples might include:

    thick grass
    hot pavement
    snow

40

a cool stream
slippery rocks
sand
gravel

Afterward, ask what they walked on that seemed most real to them. Why was that particular thing most real? One reason might be that they have strong association and recall of a specific experience. A second reason might be that more details were recalled and recreated in one of the situations. The more details one can recall, the more real it seems.

THE BEACH

Objective: To use the senses to recall being at a beach

Ask the class to find a comfortable position to sit in on the floor and to close their eyes. They are to imagine they are sitting on a log somewhere at their favorite beach. While they are imagining, sidecoach by asking questions such as the following:

What is the day like? Feel the warmth of the sun.
What sounds do you hear?
Put your hands on the ground — what are you touching?
What do you see around you?
What one thing would you like to do at the beach?
Open your eyes, trying to keep the image of the beach. Begin to do the one thing you would most like to do there.

There will be a variety of reponses. Some may just want to lie down in the sun, while some may want to go swimming, or build sand castles, or play with a frisbee.

After they have had a few moments to play, ask them what images seemed most real to them. What sounds did they hear? What beach smells did they recall?

THE ATTIC

Objective: To use the senses to imagine exploring an attic

There are two parts to this activity. The first is a warm-up for the senses. The second is a situation in which they use most of their senses in an imagined circumstance.

Part One: Tell the class that in a few minutes they are going to do something that requires concentration and keen use of the senses, so they are to practice sharpening their senses for a bit.

The sense of smell is first.
> *Close your eyes and see whether you can smell chalk, or paste or anything that might let you know you are in a classroom, just by the smell.*

Next, the sense of hearing.
> *With eyes closed, what sounds do you hear?*
> *Imagine someone is walking down the hall. Listen to the footsteps.*

Now, the sense of touch.
> *Touch something in your pocket or on your desk. Be aware of how it feels.*
> *Put it down and **imagine** you are touching it. Let your fingers remember what it felt like.*

And, the sense of sight.
> *Recall your bedroom at home, the furniture, the colors, what the floor is like.*
> *Recall what your room looks like when it is dark and all you see are big shadowy shapes.*

42

Part Two: Ask if any of them have ever been in an attic. How would they describe an attic to someone who had never heard of one before? Try to bring out descriptions that touch on each of the senses. For example, an attic might have a musty smell, be dark and full of cobwebs, have creaky floors and low ceilings, be full of boxes and trunks.

> *There is something exciting about exploring an attic, because you never know what you might find up there.*
>
> *Imagine that there is a big, old vacant house and you have decided to explore it.*
>
> *You discover it has an attic. How will you get into the attic?*
>
> *Try to get such a clear picture of the attic in your mind that you can actually **feel** the cobwebs in your face, **smell** the musty air, **hear** the creaking boards, **see** the boxes and trunks.*
>
> *At my signal, begin exploring the attic to see what you might find.*

After they have played a couple of minutes, suggest:

> *As you look around, you find something very unusual.*
>
> *Look at it carefully.*
>
> *Where could it have come from?*
>
> *What will you do with it?*

After they have played out the action, many will want to share what they found in the attic. They could either tell about it or pantomime what they found for the rest to guess. Ask what they heard or touched that made the attic seem real to them.

Other places to explore, which are rich in sensory detail, might include a cave, an old abandoned house, a thick forest.

Concept: Develop body awareness and spatial perception through *pantomime*

REACHING FOR A REASON

Objective: To stretch and reach, and pantomime activities suggested by the movement

---

Stand up and reach as high as you can.
Stretch as far to each side as you can.
Stretch as far down as you can.
Now let's give you a purpose for reaching:
    Straighten a crooked picture which is very high on the wall.
    You see some flies. Get a fly swatter and reach out to swat them.

Ask them to think of other reasons they might be stretching and reaching.

As ideas are suggested, the whole class follows through with the pantomime. Or, you might ask them to keep their ideas a secret and have five or six at a time show their ideas to the class. The class tries to determine exactly what each one is doing.

SPORTS

Objective: To pantomime their favorite outdoor sports

Divide the class into groups of five or six. Each group is to choose one outdoor sport to pantomime. They should think of the equipment they will need and how they will pantomime the sport so that the class will be able to know what it is. Give them a minute to plan.

When the groups show their sports to the rest of the class, let them play it for awhile, even if the class knows what they are doing right away. The class should look for specific actions which are appropriate to playing that sport.

DEEP SEA DIVING

Objective: To pantomime being deep sea divers on a mission

Materials: You may wish to use background music when they are diving, such as "Neptune," from *The Planets Suite,* by Holst.

First, guide the class in a warm-up, using the rhythmic movement activity called **Heavy and Light**, on page 34.

Ask if they know of any people who put weights on to do a particular activity. Give them some clues if they don't suggest deep sea divers or scuba divers. Then ask them questions such as the following:

Why do divers use weights?

What other equipment do they use?

Why do they always dive with a partner, or a "buddy"?

What are some reasons they might go diving to the bottom of the sea?

Ideas may range from finding a sunken ship to looking for specimens for scientific research.

Designate one part of the room as the boat which will take them out to sea. On that boat they will find the diving gear they need.

Each finds a buddy, and they go to the boat and help each other put on their gear.

You can play the role of the head of the expedition, who will stay on the boat once they dive off. Tell them not to put on their headgear, or helmets, until you tell them to, because after that they will not be able to talk at all. Ask them how they will communicate with their buddies under water. The answer, of course, is through pantomime.

Decide what their diving mission is, according to one of the suggestions they made earlier. As the head of the expedition, you can set the tone for the seriousness of their mission and the potential dangers. They should have some specific goal, like finding treasure, or clues about why the ship sank, or unusual specimens. When they descend, you will be the only person who can communicate with them. They jump off the boat with their buddies. (Some will probably know that they jump off the boat backwards.)

After they have played for awhile, you might communicate with them, telling them about potential danger:

My radar has picked up a dangerous object in your vicinity.

I don't know what it is. Be very careful.

After they have "conquered" the enemy, tell them your gauges show that the air supply is low, and it is time to ascend. Warn them to come up *very* slowly, so they don't get the "bends."

When all are back to the boat, they remove their gear, and share tales of their adventure.

Ask them how they communicated with their buddies.

Students may want to think of other underwater adventures. For example, they may find clues to the lost city of Atlantis, or King Neptune's Kingdom.

Concept: Develop body awareness and spatial perception through *emotional recall*

REMEMBER A TIME WHEN . . .

Objective: To recall feelings about specific incidents and act out situations revealing a particular emotional state

---

Ask the class how they are feeling right now. Answers will probably vary from "happy" to "bored." Ask them to name some other feelings they have had in the past and list them on the board.

Focus on one of the feelings, such as "mad," and ask them to recall a situation in which they were really mad.

How does your body feel when you are mad?

What kind of expression might you have on your face when you are mad?

Divide the class into small groups and assign each group a particular emotion from the list on the board. It is all right if more than one group has the same emotion. Each group is to think of a situation in which one or more of them are feeling that emotion. The groups act out their situations for the rest of the class. The class will try to determine what the feeling is.

IT DEPENDS

Objective: To do a series of actions in several different ways, depending on the situation

Ask the students to think of three different things they do when they wake up in the morning. They will repeat the same action, but the way they do it will change, depending on the situation.

1. *It is a bright, sunny day. You are feeling great and there is going to be a party at school!*

2. *It is March, and you are getting tired of school. The day is gloomy and rainy. You expect to get a test back on which you know you did poorly.*

3. *Your dog was killed the day before and you wake up remembering and missing the dog.*

4. *(In pairs) You are angry because a younger sister or brother is being a pest and has hidden the toothpaste.*

Concept: *Original dialogue*

THE LOST KITTEN

Objective: To use persuasive arguments in a given situation

They work in groups of fours. Two are the parents, and two are the children. This is the situation:

> *The two children are walking home from school on a rainy day, when they hear a little kitten meowing. They investigate, and in the bushes they find a poor bedraggled kitten, soaking wet and crying pitifully. The kitten has no identification collar. They take the kitten home and try to persuade their parents to let them keep the kitten. Previously their parents have never allowed them to have a pet for various reasons. What arguments will the parents have for not keeping it?*

They play out the scene, beginning with the finding of the kitten. While they are doing that, the parents should be at home doing whatever they might typically be doing.

After they have played for awhile, tell them they have one minute to end the scene. Will they be allowed to keep the kitten?

Afterward discuss the various arguments they came up with.

Ask students to think of other situations in which they have had to be persuasive. In groups, they can act out a situation for the rest of the class. The class can suggest other ideas they might have added to help the arguments.

THE PHONE CALL

Objective: To recognize that the tone and pitch of the voice are as expressive as the words said

Each one is to imagine telephoning a best friend. They have something very important to tell the friend. Sometime during the conversation, they are to have a big argument about something and hang up. Maybe they'll call the friend back, maybe not.

Give them a minute to think about the call and what it is they are going to tell their friends. (The friend is imagined.) Remind them to think about what their friend is saying on the other end of the phone.

Afterward ask them how their voices changed when they began to argue.

LEAVE A MESSAGE

Objective: To speak clearly and distinctly

Materials: Tape recorder and blank tape

Ask whether they have ever called someone on the telephone and heard a recorded message. Point out that sometimes people have to be away and they don't want to miss important calls, so they use the recording device.

They are to imagine that they have a recorder on their telephone at home. They are going to go somewhere after school and want to let their mothers know. They call up and give the following information:

Tell who you are,
where you will be,
how you can be reached,
when you are coming home.

Record about ten children a day and listen to the recordings to evaluate. The class will become bored if too many record on one day. Evaluate according to the clarity of the message.

50

ESSENTIAL ELEMENT TWO: CREATIVE DRAMA

Concept: Dramatize literary selections using *pantomime*

THE SORCERER'S APPRENTICE

Objective: To pantomime the action of the characters in the story

Materials: The music of *The Sorcerer's Apprentice* by Dukas

Introduce: Ask the students how many of them have to do chores around the house. Have they ever wished they could snap their fingers and the chores would all be done, or even wished they had a robot to do everything they didn't want to do?

Ask them all to become "Chore Robots" doing one thing they really dislike doing. They begin when you turn on their switches. After they have played a couple of minutes, turn their switches off and comment on some of the chores you saw them doing.

Then tell them that they are not alone in disliking some chores.

Apparently that has been true for centuries. In fact there is an old story that deals with that very subject, called *The Sorcerer's Apprentice*. Ask if anyone knows what a sorcerer is. They will find out if they are correct when they hear the story.

Present: *THE SORCERER'S APPRENTICE*

Richard Rostron

Many years ago, in far-off Switzerland, there lived a sorcerer. That is, this story took place many years ago. For all we know, the sorcerer may be living yet. His name then was Willibald, which is a little odd, but no stranger than he was. He was tall and thin, and his nose was long and pointed to match. He wore long, loose, trailing gowns. What was left of his hair was white. A small black cap sat on the back of his head.

He was not a very ordinary sorcerer. For instance, his fellow sorcerers specialized in disappearing in puffs of smoke. Then they would bob up, at a moment's notice, in places far away from where they had been a second before. But Willibald felt such tricks were beneath his dignity. To him they were a trifle show-offy. He traveled from place to place on a donkey. Of course, this took a good deal more time. But no one knew better than he did that he was no ordinary sorcerer, and that his customers would wait.

However, he did have a weakness for service. It was his habit to command pieces of furniture — chairs, tables, footstools, even brooms — to do his bidding. Of course, once in a while a passerby would be frightened out of his wits to see a table capering along the street with a bucket of water on its top. But this didn't happen often. The sorcerer lived way on the edge of town on a street that wasn't at all fashionable. And he was usually very careful not to let anyone see him work his spells. Not even Fritzl, his apprentice, knew how it was done.

Fritzl was a boy who was learning the sorcery business. He wasn't very bright or industrious. He made mistakes, spilled things, and was a general nuisance. In fact, only Willibald's patience saved him from being sent home in disgrace.

Of course, Fritzl was very pleased to have most of the unpleasant chores done for him. He didn't have to dust, or sweep, or scrub, or fetch water for the tank in the sorcerer's cellar workshop. Willibald used a good deal of water in his spells. And all this happened in the days before there were such things as faucets and sinks and city water supplies.

But in spite of all this, Fritzl wasn't satisfied. There were times when the sorcerer would go away and leave him to do all the work himself. Fritzl disliked those days terribly. So he decided to learn the spell his master used on the furniture. One day he crept to the top of the cellar stairs and peeped over. Willibald was busy stirring something in a kettle over the fire.

He stopped stirring to reach for a piece of firewood, and then exclaimed. "Out of wood again! That boy! Fritzl! *Fritzl!*"

Fritzl trembled, but didn't answer. He was afraid his master would guess that he had been spying.

52

"Fritzl! Where *is* that boy? Never here when you want him." The sorcerer grumbled a bit. Then he stopped stirring, and went over and stood a broom against the wall. He stepped back three paces, and forward two paces, and clapped his hands three times. Then he said, "Lif! Luf! Laf! Broom, fetch firewood!"

The broom immediately appeared to have arms — somewhat thin ones, and rather splintery, but still, arms. It came toward the stairs, hopping and thumping along on its straws. Willibald went back to his stirring, and Fritzl waited until the broom had thumped past his hiding place. Then he quietly crept away. Now he knew the spell, and he felt quite pleased with himself. He wouldn't have to work nearly so hard when old Willibald went off and left him to do everything alone.

There came a day when the sorcerer had to go off on business to the other side of town in a great hurry. In fact, he was almost tempted to travel in a puff of smoke instead of on his donkey. But he remembered in time who he was and soon he and his donkey were clip-clopping down the street. But before he went, he said to Fritzl:

"This place is a mess. While I'm gone you set about clearing it out. And be sure to scrub the cellar floor clean. I dropped a spell I was mixing last night, and it's left quite a large stain. I'm expecting a visitor from the Sorcerers' Society of Silesia in a few days and I don't want him to think I'm in the habit of spilling things. And then don't forget to refill the water tub in the workshop." You see, Willibald was very vain of the reputation he had of being no ordinary sorcerer.

When his master had gone, Fritzl went to work with a broom. He swept clouds of dust — both star and earth — in all directions. Then he started on the furniture, wiping and polishing till everything shone. After that he went downstairs to the workshop and scrubbed the floor there. The stain was very large and very dark, and he scrubbed a long time. By the time he had finished, the water tub was empty. It was a warm day and he had worked very hard. The idea of making many trips to the river with the water bucket didn't appeal to him at all.

Then he had an idea: Why not let the broom fetch the water? Of course, if old Willibald found out, he would very likely be terribly angry. But surely the tub would be full by the time the sorcerer returned and no one would ever know. So Fritzl thought, and he wasted no time in thinking any further.

He seized the broom, stood it up against the wall, stepped back three paces, forward two paces, as he had seen Willibald do, then clapped his hands three times and said the magic words: "Lif! Luf! Laf! Broom, fetch water from the river!" He was delighted when the broom's arms appeared and it picked up the water bucket and started — thump-athump-athump! — up the stairs.

Soon it was back, and before Fritzl knew what was happening, it had tilted the bucket and flung the water across the room with a splash. Then it was off again — a thump-athump! before Fritzl could stop it.

The water ran about and got in Fritzl's shoes, which wasn't very comfortable. He thought: "Well, perhaps I didn't think fast enough. When it comes back I'll make it put the water in the tub instead of spilling it out on the floor."

Almost before he knew it. The broom had returned. As soon as it appeared at the top of the stairs with another bucket of water, Fritzl called out: "Don't throw it. Pour it in the tub!" But the broom paid no heed, flung the water as before, and went off — thump-athump-athump! — for more.

Poor Fritzl was frantic. "Something is wrong here," he thought. "Perhaps I'd better do the job myself and not try to get it done by magic. And when the broom returned again, he clapped his hands three times and cried: "Lif! Luf! Laf! Broom, stop fetching water!" But once more the broom paid no heed and flung the water across the room. And again it went off — thump-athump-athump! for more.

Again and again the broom went back and forth, each time fetching and sloshing out a bucket of water and returning to the river for another. Fritzl became desperate. The water rose higher and higher until it reached his knees. Everything — even the big water tub — started floating around the room. And Fritzl's panic grew and grew. At last he seized an ax and next time the broom came with a bucket of water, he swung wildly and split it down the middle. But instead of stopping, the two pieces went merrily on. Each piece grew another arm, and another bucket appeared from nowhere. Off they went — thump-athump-athump! — to the river.

Higher and higher the flood mounted. The two brooms came and went faster and faster. Fritzl wept and pleaded. He repeated snatches of spells he had heard his master use. He tried to get out of the cellar, but the water had floated the wooden steps out of place. The brooms went on and on and the water rose and rose.

54

Just as it rose to his chin, Fritzl heard the clip-clop of his master's donkey coming along the street. Then he heard the donkey stop and Willibald coming in the front door. "Help! Help!" he cried.

Willibald quickly appeared at the top of the stairs. "What goes on here?" he howled. Just then the brooms came in with more water and sloshed it down the stairs. Willibald was in the way and his gown was drenched. And there is nothing quite so angry as a wet sorcerer.

"Help, Master, quick!" poor Fritzl wailed. "I tried to make the broom fetch water, and then it wouldn't stop. Do something, before I drown!"

"Dumbhead!" roared Wilibald. "I ought to let you drown. It's just what you deserve!" As he said this, he jumped hastily aside, for the brooms could be heard thump-athump-athump!-ing into the house. When they appeared, the sorcerer clapped his hand *four* times. Then he gabbled a long string of words. But Fritzl didn't hear them, for just then the water tub bumped against his head. He lost his footing and went under the water with a gurgle.

Next thing he knew, he was lying on the floor coughing and gasping. He looked around him. The water was gone. In fact, there wasn't anything in the cellar that was even wet. The steps were back in their places in the stairs. One broom stood quietly and peacefully in the woodbox, with a bucket beside it. The other broom and bucket had disappeared.

Fritzl looked fearfully up at his master. The sorcerer stood at the top of the stairs, sputtering and fuming with rage. "Get out of my sight, you blockhead! I've reached the end of my patience! Go on, get out! Go back where you came from!" And he clapped his hands quite a bit and stamped his foot — the left one — and a puff of smoke appeared on the floor beside Fritzl.

The puff of smoke grew and grew. As it grew it moved over and covered the apprentice. He shut his eyes in fright. He felt himself being lifted and heard a whistling in his ears like the wind. Then he was dropped with a hard bump. When he opened his eyes, he saw he was in his mother's front yard.

Fritzl lived to be a very old man, but he never saw the sorcerer again. And he didn't want to. In the fine summer evenings he would sit and tell stories to his grandchildren. They liked best the story of old Willibald and the broom. They remembered it and told it to their grandchildren. And *they* told it to *their* grandchildren. And so it has come down to us.

Plan: Discuss Fritzl's feelings and reactions from the time he is left alone to do all the work through to Willibald's return.

Act: Then ask them all to imagine they are Fritzl, after Willibald has gone. They go through the actions while you sidecoach or repeat that portion of the story. Use the music as background.

Plan: Ask them how they could create the broom which doubles. Have some students demonstrate.

Talk about Willibald, and what he was like.

How did he feel about Fritzl to begin with?

How did he feel when he came back?

Other characters in the story could include various pieces of furniture which bob around in all the water.

Review the story, and then cast the characters. You may want to have half the class play while the other half acts as audience.

Act: The students may feel confident enough to use their own words. If not, you can narrate from the time that Fritzl decides to spy on Willibald. You will notice that the recording is much longer than the story. Choose the portion you feel is best suited to the action.

Evaluate: Talk about how the characters helped create the mounting tension in the story. Ask how they might make the story even better. Then let those who were the audience the first time act out the story.

Concept: Dramatize literary selections using *improvisation* which leads to an understanding of *plot structure*

THE BAD JOKE THAT ENDED WELL

Objective: To use improvisation to enact a story that has a clear beginning, middle, climax and ending

---

Introduce: Ask the children about various ways they solve problems. Think of some problems that they might be able to relate to. For example:

It is a rainy afternoon and you want to watch a certain television show and someone else in your family wants to watch a different show. If you have only one television set, how would you solve the problem?

Or, you want to play soccer, but nobody will choose you for a team.

The story for today is about some people who have a problem. Tell the children to listen for what the problem is and how they tried to solve it.

Present: *THE BAD JOKE THAT ENDED WELL*

Roger Duvoisin

In a certain little town in French Switzerland things were going very badly. The communal forest was fast becoming bare of trees and the communal chest bare of money. The people found the taxes too high, and complained that they got nothing in return. It was a sad state of affairs. The Council scratched their heads over the council table, and finally came to the conclusion that such a desperate situation required a desperate remedy. After much discussion a remedy was hit upon. Perhaps it was a good one, perhaps not, but in any case they actually made a decision.

And what was the decision?

It was this. The next town was as well run as this town was poorly run. Surely the Council in that next town must be made up of very wise men. Undoubtedly it would be a good thing to ask their advice. They might even be induced to part with some of their wisdom. Was not that a good idea? The Council thought so.

The next day they departed: the Mayor carrying an empty bag under his arm, followed by his Councilmen and the Clerk. It was hot, and the grass bordering the side of the winding road was covered with dust, but still, it was a fine day.

Noon had come by the time the Council entered the Town Hall of the next town. The Clerk there bade them be seated.

"Pray, Mr. Mayor and Gentlemen, to what good fortune do we owe the great honor of your visit?"

The Mayor cleared his throat and explained.

"Mr. Clerk, the whole world knows and admires the administration of your town. You must indeed be wise men. And we have come to seek your advice, and beg you to spare us some of your wisdom. We greatly need it. See. I have brought a bag for it." The Mayor here hopefully unfolded the bag.

The Clerk was rather amazed, but he was also quick-witted. The empty bag gave him an idea.

"Gentlemen," he said, smiling and rubbing his hands together, "we are proud of your request and shall do our best to help you. If you will give me your bag, it will take but a moment to put the Spirit of Wisdom into it."

The Clerk ran into the garden behind the Town Hall. Making sure that he was not seen, he managed to detach a wasp's nest which hung from the pear tree. He put it in the bag and carefully tied the strings.

"Mr. Mayor," he said as he re-entered, "I think I have what you want. Here is the Spirit of Wisdom, in the bag. Keep it carefully until you reach your town. Do not be disturbed if it seems to move, or make humming, buzzing sounds. That will be a good sign; a sign that the Spirit is very much alive. When you get home go into your Council Room. Close the door and all the shutters. Then shake the bag and open it. I can assure you, gentlemen, that almost at once you will feel the effect."

"Mr. Clerk," said the Mayor, rising from his chair, "we thank you from the bottom of our hearts."

With light feet the Council started home. The Mayor tied the bag to his blue umbrella, and carried it over his shoulder. He was proud to bear this precious and historic burden.

The wasps soon began to stir and buzz inside the bag. It was music to the Council's ears.

"Hear it?" asked the delighted Mayor. "Ah! What a good little Spirit we have here."

"Lively as a kitten," said the President.

It was late when the Council reached their town. Some peasants were already returning from the fields, the men balancing their forks and scythes over their shoulders, and the women, in black bodices and wide sleeves, carrying the lunch baskets.

The Mayor and his Council proceeded importantly to the Town Hall and the bag was deposited upon the council table. The door and shutters were tightly closed. The Council took their seats.

It was a solemn moment. The Council fully felt its importance as they waited in silence for the Mayor to untie the bag, which he did, after shaking it vigorously two or three times.

A low distant murmur, the chant of Wisdom, was heard. It grew and grew until it became a furious buzzing and the Spirit began to inoculate its Wisdom. It was a burning inoculation.

"I've got the Spirit on the nose!" shouted the Mayor. "Ouch! On the lips, on the neck too!"

"I have it on the cheeks!" cried the President.

"It stung me on the forehead!" said the Vice-President. "What a lively Spirit!"

"Ouch!" yelled the Clerk, "it just came in through my chin!"

"And me! Good heavens!" shouted a Councilman. "I have it everywhere!"

Only when the buzzing and the stinging seemed to lessen did the Council, feeling that the Spirit of Wisdom had penetrated deeply enough, open the shutters.

What a sight! They hardly knew each other. Their faces were red and swollen beyond recognition. And all around the Council Room and over the table the Spirit of Wisdom was flying and crawling.

"Wasps!" yelped the Council.

"The rascal! It's a joke!" cried the Mayor.

"We have been cheated," wept the President.

But no. They had not been cheated. The neighboring Clerk would never have believed it, but the Spirit of Wisdom bore its fruit. The Council learned that to have a well-ordered town, they must count on themselves. When they recovered from their pains and swellings (which they hid as best they could), they went to work as they had never done before. Their town became a model of good administration.

Plan: First, discuss the story in terms of plot. You may want to chart the various parts on the chalkboard.

Usually, the *beginning* of any story states a problem of some kind.

What was the basic problem?

The way a story *ends* relates to the problem in some way.

How did this story end, in terms of the problem?

The *middle* of the story tells how the characters go about trying to solve the problem.

In this story, how did the Council try to solve the problem?

Before the end of the story, there is usually an exciting part that is called the *climax*.

What was the climax of this story?

Discuss the climax scene in more detail, beginning with the Mayor and the Council entering their council room, closing the doors and windows, and taking their seats around the table.

How did they feel when they sat down?

When the bag was first opened, did they realize that the stinging was caused by wasps? What did they think?

When did they finally realize what had happened?

Act: The entire class can improvise the action and dialogue of the Mayor and the Council members. Or have half the class do it first, followed by the other half who can make any changes they wish.

Evaluate: Talk about parts of the improvisation which clearly showed how the characters felt about the stings before *and* after they realized the cause. Ask the children to summarize the four parts of a story.

APPLICATION OF PLOT

Objective: To show understanding of the four parts of a plot by improvising original stories

Introduce: Review the parts of a plot as discussed in the previous lesson.

Plan: Divide the class into small groups of three or four. Give each group a beginning and indicate the problem. They are to decide on a middle, a climax, and an ending. They may add as many characters to their scene as they have in their group. The following are suggestions for scenes, but feel free to construct your own.

1. You open the closet door and all the clothes are gone.
2. Your father told you not to swim too far from shore.
3. You are hiking up a steep mountain path and one of you stumbles and injures a leg.
4. You are playing baseball and the ball hits an old lady and knocks her down.
5. You take your new bicycle to school against the advice of your parents.
6. You take something very valuable to school to show the class, and lose it.
7. You call your dog for dinner and he doesn't come.
8. You told on somebody and now no one will play with you.

Allow a few minutes for planning and trying out the scenes.

Act and Evaluate: The scenes can be acted for the class audience. After each scene, ask the audience to identify the beginning, middle, climax and end. This may take two days to complete.

Concept: Dramatize literary selections emphasizing the
physical attributes of characterization

THE STONE IN THE ROAD

Objective: To use posture, gestures and movements which show
the physical characteristics of the people portrayed

Introduce: Discuss a hypothetical situation with the class, such as the
following:

> *Suppose you wanted to be really nice to your family, so you cooked
> all the meals, cleaned up the dishes, cleaned the house, and brought
> your family whatever they wanted when they wanted it. You did
> this not for one day, but everyday for weeks.*
>
> *Your family was delighted, and soon they didn't even offer to help,
> they just let you do everything. In fact, if you were at all slow when
> they called you to do something, they got angry. How would that
> make you feel, when you were trying to please them?*

Tell them that that situation isn't too different from something that
happened in a particular story.

As they listen, they should try to get a picture in their minds of what the
various characters are doing and what they look like.

Present: *THE STONE IN THE ROAD*

> There was once a Duke who lived in a fine house on the edge of a
> little village. He was kind and generous to the village folk, and many
> a time he helped them when they were in trouble.
>
> If the wind blew the roof off a man's barn, the Duke would send his
> servants to help him build another. If there was illness and distress
> in the town, he could be counted on to help unfortunate families.
> When crops were poor, the villagers could be sure that he would not
> let them go hungry.
>
> As the years passed, however, the Duke realized that people relied

too much on his generosity. They were becoming more and more lazy, and instead of being grateful, they were envious and discontented. He resolved, therefore, to test them to find out whether there were not at least a few villagers who would exert themselves for the good of others. He hoped in this way to make the people see themselves as they really were.

One morning very early he went out to the highway and pushed a large stone into the very middle of the road. He had to tug and pull with all his might, but he would allow no one to help him. Just before he pushed it into place, he took from under his cloak a bag of gold, and dropping it to the ground, he covered it with the stone. Then he went behind a nearby hedge to watch what might happen.

Before long a farmer came along, driving some sheep to market. He could scarcely believe his eyes when he saw the big stone blocking the way.

"Run ahead, lad," he said to his son, "and see if it is really a stone." For it was only beginning to be light, and he thought it might be something that had fallen out of an ox-cart.

"It *is* a stone, father," said the boy after he had explored. "How ever could it have come there?"

"Well, one thing is sure," replied the farmer. "*We'll* not try to move it. Let the Duke's servants get it out of the way." And with the help of the boy, he drove the sheep around the stone, grumbling all the while about the trouble it caused him.

Before long, two country women came along, carrying baskets of eggs to sell. They were so busy talking about the price they hoped to get for their eggs and wishing that it would be enough to pay for the cloth for a new dress that when they saw the stone they did not at first appear to be surprised. Indeed, one of them sat on it to pull up the heel of her shoe, and discovering that she was somewhat tired, she decided to sit until she was rested. Only then did it occur to the second woman that she had never seen a stone here before.

"Why, a carriage could never get around this thing," she said. "I wonder that the Duke leaves it here!"

But her companion, resting on its broad surface, was dreaming of the fine clothes she would have if she were rich like the Duke's lady. She could not know that well within her reach was a tidy sum of money that would buy more dresses than she could wear in a lifetime.

Hour after hour a procession of people passed along the busy highway, some scolding about the stone, others enjoying the novelty

63

of it, but none offering to move it out of the road. There were laborers, well-to-do merchants, soldiers; some proud ladies who were turned back because there was not room for their carriage to pass; a scholar, so deep in his reading that he stumbled over the stone; a peddler, a minstrel, a beggar.

The Duke had all but given up hope when, about dusk, he heard a gay whistle in the distance. It came from the miller's son, who was trudging along the road with a heavy sack of meal over his shoulder. Suddenly the whistling stopped.

"A stone in the middle of the road!" he said to himself. "That's a queer place for a stone as big as that! Someone will fall over it!" And in less time than it takes to tell about it, he had put his sack of meal on the ground and shoved the stone off the road. As he went back to get the meal, he saw the bag of gold.

"Somebody has lost this," he thought. But no sooner had he picked it up than the Duke stepped out from his hiding-place.

"Read what is written on the bag, my boy," he said.

"For him who moves the stone," read the astonished lad. "Then —?"

"It is for you," said the Duke kindly. "I am glad to find that there is one person in our village who is willing to go to some trouble out of thoughtfulness for others."

"Oh, thank you, thank you, sir!" cried the boy. "It was a little thing to do! You are very kind!" And off he sped to tell his mother of his wonderful good fortune.

Plan: There are a number of characters mentioned in the story, plus many others that could be added to the story. Ask which ones they can remember from the story. After they name a character, ask how they imagine that person walking down the road.

> *What does the person look like?*
> *What posture?*
> *How does the person hold his/her head?*

Try out some of the characters by showing how they would move:

> the proud ladies,
> the scholar,
> the beggar,
> the soldiers.

Ask them what other interesting characters might come down the road and react in different ways to the stone, but not move it. For example, maybe a mother and her children see the stone and decide to eat their lunch on it. Or an artist comes by and decides to paint it.

Divide the class into groups of three or four. The task of each group is to encounter the stone in some way, playing certain kinds of characters. The way they move and act should help show what kind of characters they are. Allow them a few minutes to plan and to try out their characters. They may talk in character, as well.

Act: Establish where the stone is. Maybe a large table could be used as the stone. Each group enters, one at a time to encounter the stone. While one group is playing, the others should watch to see how the characters move to show who they are.

Evaluate: Discuss what they did, emphasizing the way the physical attributes helped reveal what the characters were like.

Concept: Dramatize literary selections emphasizing the *objectives of the characters*

THE WIND AND THE SUN

Objective: To clearly show the characters' objectives, or reasons,

---

Introduce: Divide the class into groups of five or six. Present the following riddle. In their groups they are to decide on an answer for the riddle, and develop some movements which will show what the answer is without telling it outloud.

> *What flies forever*
> *And rests never? (Answer: the wind.)*

Each group shows their answer to the rest of the class. Afterward, ask them which answer most closely fits the riddle. They will probably arrive at the correct response. If not, tell them.

> *Suppose that two people are arguing about which of them is the stronger.*
> *How might they prove who is stronger?*

They might fight; they might have a contest to see who could lift the heaviest weights.

Tell them there is an old fable in which two characters were arguing about who was stronger. One character was the wind and one was the sun.

Present: *THE WIND AND THE SUN*

    Wind and Sun had an argument one day, about which was the stronger.

    "I am the stronger." boasted Wind, puffing out his cheeks and blowing so hard that every leaf on the trees shook. "You sit up there, Sun, and do nothing but shine — that is, when I don't blow the clouds across the sky. When *that* happens, you can't even be seen! Of course I'm the stronger."

66

"Don't be too sure," answered Sun calmly, filling the air with his warm radiance. "I'll tell you what. We'll have a contest, shall we?"

"Certainly," said Wind. "Then everyone will know, once and for all, who is the stronger. What shall the contest be?"

"See that fellow over there?" said Sun, gazing across the countryside toward a winding, white road. Along it walked a traveller with a cloak about his shoulders.

"I see him," said Wind.

"Well then, let's see which of us can get his cloak off first."

"With all my heart!" agreed Wind. "That's easy. I'll have his cloak off his back in no time."

So saying, he began to blow. Phoo-oo-oo! The traveller on the road took no notice. But Wind had scarcely begun. He blew harder, and then harder still, until the water of the lakes turned to great waves, and the trees were bent almost double, and the birds in the air were dashed hither and thither with the force of the gale. But the traveller, instead of taking his cloak off, only held it closer around him; and the harder Wind blew, the tighter he clutched it. It was no good. Even when Wind roared like a thousand demons, and blew so as to snap the branches from the stoutest oaks, he could not get the traveller's cloak off his back. At last Wind was tired out and could blow no more.

It was Sun's turn. By now the sky was all covered over with dark storm-clouds, but as soon as Wind stopped blowing they gently drifted apart, and Sun shone warmly down over the green fields. Warmer and warmer grew the air under his pleasant beams, and soon the traveller unbuttoned his cloak and let it hang loosely about him. Thanks to Sun's kindly heat he was soon glad to take if off altogether and carry it over his arm.

"There!" said Sun. "Which of us got it off — tell me that."

Wind only growled and said nothing. But he knew he was beaten. Sun was the stronger after all.

GENTLENESS DOES MORE THAN VIOLENCE.

Plan: The story opens before the contest has been decided on, with the wind and the sun arguing about who is the stronger.

How might you show that argument?

What might the wind and sun be doing when they argue?

One possibility is to have the sun and wind alternately show what they can do — perhaps getting madder each time until the contest is set.

   Divide the class into groups to have them work out the opening argument. Some can be the wind and the sun, some can show the effects of the wind and the sun's action. Ask them to think about what kind of voices the wind and sun might have. They are to end the opening argument by deciding to have a contest.

Act: Each group acts out the opening argument.

Evaluate: Discuss their work, talking about the best ideas from each. Then choose ideas from each which would make the best opening.

Plan: Plan the contest.

> *What is the objective, or purpose, of the wind? The sun?*
> *Both have the same objective: to prove who is the stronger.*
> *How does the wind feel when the man begins to tighten his cloak? What does he do?*
> *What is the sun doing in the meantime?*
> *What other characters might be in the play to help indicate the strength of the wind?*
> *How do you want to end the play?*

Cast the parts.

Act: Some students may want to make the sound effects of the wind, while others act it out.

Evaluate: Ask what parts of the play were believable. Were the objectives of the wind and sun clear? What could to done to strengthen the play?

APPLICATION OF CHARACTER OBJECTIVES

Objective: To show they understand that a character always has an objective, a reason for his or her action.

Introduce: Ask:

Why does a bird listen to the ground?

Why does a dog bark?

Why do you knock on a door?

Why do you raise your hand in class?

*Everything we do, we do for a reason or a purpose. Another word for purpose is **objective**.*

Imagine that you go into your room and close the door. What might be your reason — your objective? Maybe your objective is to be alone, because you are angry; maybe it is to get away from your younger brother; maybe it is to hide a birthday present.

Imagine you are baking a cake, what might be your objective? Your objective is the reason why you do something.

Plan: Divide the class into pairs or threes. Give each group a card with a character and action on it and a blank for the objective. The group decides what the objective is.

For example:

Character	Action	Objective
Mother	calls her son	

There are a number of possible objectives: to run an errand; to clean up his room; to eat dinner; to answer the phone. The group decides on one of the objectives to act out.

A list of characters and actions follows. You may wish to add others, or, after the class works with the idea for awhile, they could make up their own lists.

Character	Action	Objective
1. Boy or girl	throws a rope out from a boat	
2. Cat	stalks a mouse	
3. Boy or girl	listens to a record	
4. Young child	rides a bike	
5. Boy or girl	skates	
6. Boy or girl	washes a car	
7. Boy or girl	looks in a drawer	
8. Boy or girl	hides	
9. Boy or girl	walks on tiptoe	
10. Boy or girl	paints a picture	
11. Dog	whines and whimpers	
12. Grandparent	reads outloud	

Act: Each group should have several turns. Those who are watching are to try to determine both the action and the objective being played.

Evaluate: Those watching try to determine the objective of the character's action. Was the objective clear? If not, how could they clarify it?

Concept: Dramatize literary selections using *original dialogue*

THE WISE PEOPLE OF GOTHAM

Objective: To improvise the dialogue in the story

Introduce: Ask the children what it means to "use your wits." Ask if they can think of an example, either from their own experience or from something they have seen on television. There are many times in life when a person has to use his or her wits. An old folk tale tells of some very unusual ways the people in a certain town used their wits.

Present: *THE WISE PEOPLE OF GOTHAM*

One day, news was brought to Gotham that the king was coming that way, and that he would pass through the town. This did not please the men of Gotham at all, for they knew that the king was a cruel, bad man. If he came to their town, they would have to find food and lodging for him and his men: and if he saw anything that pleased him, he would be sure to take it for his own. What should they do?

They met together to talk the matter over.

"Let us chop down the big trees in the woods, so that they will block up the highway that leads into town," said one of the wise men.

"Good!" said all the rest.

So they went out with their axes, and soon the highway that led to the town was filled with logs and brush. The king's horsemen would have a hard time of it getting into Gotham.

When the king came, and saw that the road had been blocked, he was very angry.

"Who chopped those trees down in my way?" he asked of two country lads that were passing by.

"The men of Gotham," said the lads.

"Well," said the king, "go and tell the men of Gotham that I shall come with my sheriff into their town and have all their noses cut off."

71

The two lads ran to the town as fast as they could, and made known what the king had said.

Everybody was in a great fright. The men ran from house to house, carrying the news, and asking one another what they should do.

"Our wits have kept the king out of the town," said one, "and so now our wits must save our noses."

"True, true!" said the others. "But what shall we do?"

Then one, whose name was Dobbin, and who was thought to be the wisest of them all, said, "Let me tell you something. Many a man has been punished because he was wise, but I have never heard of anyone being harmed because he was a fool. So, when the king's sheriff comes, let us all act like fools."

"Good, good!" cried the others. "We will all act like fools."

It was no easy thing for the king's men to open the road; but after a time they succeeded in doing so. Just before they reached the town, they saw a queer sight. Some old men were rolling big stones up the hill, and all the young men were looking on, and grunting very loudly.

The king stopped the horses, and asked what they were doing.

"We are rolling stones uphill to make the sun rise," said one of the old men.

"You foolish fellow!" said the king. "Don't you know that the sun will rise without any help?"

"Ah, will it?" said the old man. "Well, I never thought of that. How wise you are!"

"And what are *you* doing?" said the sheriff to the young men.

"Oh, we do the grunting while our fathers do the working," they answered.

"I see," said the sheriff. "Well, that is the way the world goes everywhere." And they rode on toward the town.

They soon came to a field where a number of people were building a stone wall.

"What are you doing?" asked the king.

"Why, master," they answered, "there is a cuckoo in this field, and we are building a wall around it so as to keep the bird from straying away."

"You foolish people!" said the king. "Don't you know that the bird will fly over the top of your wall no matter how high you build it?"

"Why, no," they said. "We never thought of that. How very wise you are!"

72

They next met a man who was carrying a door on his back.

"What are you doing?" the sheriff asked.

"I have just started on a long journey," said the man.

"But why do you carry that door?" asked the sheriff.

"I left my money at home."

"Then why didn't you leave the door at home too?"

"I was afraid of thieves; and you see, if I have the door with me, they can't break it open and get in."

"You foolish fellow!" said the sheiff. "It would be safer to leave the door at home, and carry the money with you."

"Ah, would it though?" said the man. "Now, I never thought of that. You are the wisest man that I ever saw."

Then the king and the sheriff rode on with the men; but every one that they met was doing some silly thing. Soon the king and his men were all laughing.

"Truly, I believe that the people of Gotham are all fools," said one of the horsemen.

"That is true," said another. "It would be a shame to harm such simple people."

"Let us ride back to London," said the king. "They are too stupid to punish."

So they all rode back to the city and never bothered the people of Gotham again.

Plan: Discuss the story.

How did the people of Gotham use their wits?
Which example seemed the most foolish to you?

Try out the situation of the old men rolling big stones up the hill, while the young men grunted. Half the class can be the old men, half, the young men. You act the role of the King who talks to them, asking what on earth they are doing.

Ask them to think of other foolish things that could be added to the story. The whole class can work on this, or they can work in groups.

Select the best ideas and use those, along with the ones in the story. Assign each group an idea to work with.

Act: Some can play the soldiers of the king, who encounter the various groups of people. In order to give them more opportunity for dialogue, it would be helpful for you to play the king, or the King's chancellor, who asks questions of the people.

Evaluate: Discuss what they did. Could they have talked more to the king? Did their conversation show how "dumb" but respectful they were?

Concept: Dramatize literary selections using
shadow play and puppetry

THE STRANGE VISITOR

Objective: To construct the shadow puppets and act out the story

Materials: Lightweight cardboard;

Scissors, masking tape, heavy thread or fine wire, paper fasteners, hole punch;

Rods, made from dowels, skewer sticks, straws, hangers, etc;

A large, heavy cardboard box, such as an appliance box;

A white sheet, or other white material, as wrinkle-free as possible;

Two lamps, 100 or 150 watts;

Translucent materials such as colored cellephane, 1/16 in. sheet plastic which can be painted, or gauze;

Music with an eerie sound, such as "Adagio," from *Music for Strings, Percusion and Celesta,* by Bartok.

Introduce: Play the music. Ask the children what kind of mood the music creates. Among the answers will be the word "mysterious," or a similar word. Ask the children to move their hands in a mysterious way to the music. Then tell them to get up slowly and move their whole bodies to the mysterious music.

Tell them you know a story that is just as mysterious as the music. It is about an old woman who is sitting by a spinning wheel, spinning. Describe, or ask the children to describe, how a spinning wheel works.

Present: *THE STRANGE VISITOR*

Adapted from an English fairy tale

A woman, alone, sat spinning one night.
She sat, and she spun.
So alone.

75

A gust of wind; the door opened.
No one there?
Mmmm.

In came a pair of broad, broad feet
And sat themselves down by the fireside.

A woman, so lonely, sat spinning that night.
    She sat, and she spun.
    Was she alone?

In came a pair of long, long legs.
    Sat themselves down on the broad, broad feet.

The woman, so lonely, sat spinning that night.
    She sat, and she spun.
    Was she alone?

In came a body, so round that it whirled.
Sat itself down on the long, long legs.

The woman, so lonely, sat spinning that night.
    She sat, and she spun.
    All alone?

In came a pair of waving arms.
Sat themselves down on the body.

The woman, so lonely, sat spinning that night.
    She sat, and she spun.
    All alone?

In came a head; it wobbled and lurched.
On top of the waving arms it perched.

The woman, so lonely, stopped spinning that night.
She looked at the creature.
Her voice choked with fright.

"How did you get such broad, broad feet?"
      (The creature responded, and I repeat,)
      "From much walking, from much walking."

"How did you get such long, long legs?"
      "From wandering the earth
      To see what it's worth."

"How did you get such a round, round body?"
      "From chasing in circles,
      Unending circles."
"How did you get such long, waving arms?"
      "From swinging the sickle,
      The axe and the sickle."

"How did you get such a wobbly head?"
      "It's held by a thread
      Waiting to be fed."

"But, what did you come for?"
      "Come for?
            YOU!"

brad together

overlap separate arms and legs

CONSTRUCT:

Shadow puppets are really silhouettes. Sometimes they are made entirely of lightweight cardboard, which will make the figures appear all black when they are placed behind the screen. Sometimes parts of the figures are cut out and colored cellophane is taped in, which will show up when behind the screen.

For this story, you may want to have all the figures solid, except for the fire in the fireplace, where the flames could be red and yellow. If you think the parts of the body would be more ominous with color added, that is also a possibility.

The puppets should be in proportion to each other, of course. A general rule of thumb is to make them about 12″ for easy manipulation and viewing by the audience.

Tape hinge and straw

THE OLD WOMAN:

She should be hinged at the hips, so she can move forward and backward when she is spinning.

1. Make the hinge by overlapping the two parts of the body. Punch a hole in both parts and loosely insert a paper fastener (brad), so the parts can move easily.

2. Attach a rod to the middle of the figure. If you use a straw for the rod, fasten it with a masking tape hinge. If you use a different rod, tape a paper clip to one end. Attach it to the figure with a brad, or by "sewing" thin wire on the figure and inserting the paper clip.

BODY PARTS:

Each part will need a rod attached. The feet are two figures, which move separately, but both can be operated by one puppeteer. The same is true for the legs and arms. For the head, cut out facial features to make them show up.

Use separate rods for all body parts.

78

fold
flap
to box floor

SCENERY:

You will need a spinning wheel, a chair, and a fireplace. The "door" is offstage. The scenery is stationary and can be attached to the inside frame of the stage, by hanging it with thread from the top and making a flap that can be taped down to the floor of the stage.

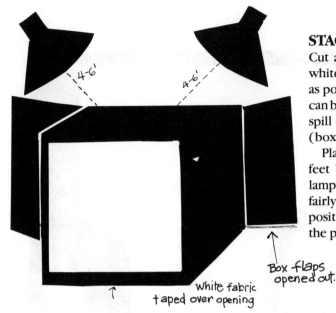

4-6'

4-6'

Box flaps
opened out.

white fabric
taped over opening

STAGE:

Cut a rectangle in a large, heavy box. Fasten the white material to the inside of the opening as tightly as possible. Leave the sides on the box, so the box can be placed on a table and so that the light will not spill out the sides. Decorate the front of the stage (box), if you wish.

Place two 100 or 150 watt lamps about four to six feet behind the screen on each side. Focus the lamps slightly downward, to distribute the light fairly evenly across the screen. If the lights are positioned correctly, there will be no shadows from the puppeteers themselves.

Act: Each puppet moves as indicated by the story and when it talks. The puppets should generally be very close to the screen for everything they do. When the individual body parts speak, they should move in some way. Each part might take a "step" toward the back of the stage when it speaks, momentarily disassociated from the rest of the body until the head completes it again. Moving backward will make it appear larger. At the end, "Come for? YOU!" the body could "lunge" toward the old woman and then both of them could fly all the way backward until they disappear. Experiment with the effects until the class finds one it likes.

This particular story is an excellent one for choral reading. Several children might want to practice it until they achieve the mood they want.

The Bartok music also adds a lot to this story.

Evaluate: Talk about how the puppets, scenery, voices and music helped create the mood. Is there any way the story could be even more scary?

Introduce: There is nothing more annoying than a mosquito! This West African legend explains how the mosquito came to be such a nuisance.

Present: *WHY MOSQUITOES BUZZ IN PEOPLE'S EARS*

Adapted by Monica Michell

One lazy afternoon, Mosquito saw Iguana napping in the sun. "Wake up, Iguana," said Mosquito. "I have a joke to tell you."

"Go away, don't bother me!" grumbled Iguana. "I am trying to sleep, and besides, I have already heard all your silly jokes."

Mosquito would not go away. He kept pestering Iguana. Finally, Iguana stuck two sticks in his ears and lumbered off through the tall grass.

Python saw Iguana coming. "Good day, Iguana," called the snake. Iguana did not answer, he did not even nod his head. "Oh no!" thought Python. "Iguana must be angry with me. I fear he is plotting some mischief against me. I'd better find a place to hide." Python looked about nervously and slithered into a nearby rabbit hole.

When Rabbit saw the big snake coming into her burrow, she was terrified. She hopped out the back way and scurried into the rain forest as fast as she could scamper.

Monkey was sitting in a tall tree eating a banana. He saw Rabbit running for her life and figured that some dangerous beast was chasing her. Monkey dropped his banana and began leaping about and screeching a warning to the other animals in the forest. In his excitement, Monkey happened to step on an old, rotten tree limb. It

81

broke and fell with a crash on Mother Owl's nest, killing one of her owlets.

"Oh, my poor precious baby," wept Mother Owl. All the rest of that day and all through the night Mother Owl sat in her tree and cried. Her sorrow was unbearable.

Now everyone knows that it is Mother Owl's job to wake the sun each morning. But, after crying all night, Mother Owl could not manage even one small hoot. So, the sun slept on and darkness lingered.

The animals began to fear that the sun would never shine again. They decided to call on the Great Spirit for help. "Oh, Great Spirit, help us please! The sun won't come up and we can't see!"

All of a sudden, lightning crackled in the sky and thunder shook the earth. The animals waited in suspense. Then, the Great Spirit appeared before the assembled animals and roared, "What seems to be the problem?"

"Mother Owl won't wake the sun," the animals chorused.

"Mother Owl," said the Great spirit sternly, "Why haven't you hooted to wake the sun?"

"I have been crying all night and half the day," sobbed Mother Owl. "Monkey killed one of my precious owlets."

"I didn't mean to," said Monkey nervously. "I saw Rabbit running for her life and tried to help spread the alarm."

"Please don't blame me," whispered the trembling Rabbit. "Python chased me out of my own home."

"It wasn't my fault," hissed Python. "I was only trying to hide from Iguana."

The Great Spirit glared at Iguana. "Well, Iguana, what do you have to say for yourself?"

Iguana just blinked. Then he remembered the sticks in his ears and quickly pulled them out. "Excuse me, Sir. Would you mind repeating the question?" asked Iguana politely.

"What mischief are you plotting against Python?" demanded the Great Spirit. "Why did you not say 'Good day' to him?"

"I am not plotting any mischief against my friend, Python," answered the bewildered Iguana. "And, I did not greet him because I did not hear him. I put these sticks in my ears because Mosquito was pestering me with his ridiculous jokes."

The Great Spirit looked at each animal one by one. "Hmmmmmm," he said. "Let me see if I've got this straight. Mother Owl's baby was killed by Monkey who was alarmed by Rabbit who was startled by Python who was frightened by Iguana who was buzzed at and bothered by that pesky Mosquito."

"That's right!" shouted all the animals.

"So it seems," said the Great Spirit ominously, that Mosquito is the culprit! Bring him here to me. Mosquito shall be punished!"

Then the Great Spirit turned to Mother Owl and said kindly. "When you return to your nest, you will find that I have restored your precious baby back to life."

Mother Owl was overjoyed! She hooted her thanks and she hooted her joy and the sun came up at last!

But the animals never did find Mosquito, for he had hidden deep in the forest. So, Mosquito never got the punishment he deserved. To this day, Mosquito has a guilty conscience. That is why he goes about whining and buzzing in people's ears: "Mmmzzzmm! Is everyone still angry at me?"

CONSTRUCT:

In West Africa, the village storytellers sometimes use elaborate masks and costumes to act out their stories. The special kind of costume described here is called a body puppet. The body puppet is almost as big as the person wearing it, and is worn, like a costume, hanging from a string around the neck.

There are a number of characters in the story. Others can be added, or several children can play monkeys, pythons and rabbits.

1. Each child decides what character to play and decides how it should look.

2. Use a paper plate, a box or a cardboard cutout to make the puppet's head. Use paper scraps, crayons or felt markers to design the puppet's face.

3. Make the body out of butcher paper, shopping bags, fabric remnants or old pillowcases. Color or paint the puppet's body to suit the character.

4. Create legs, arms and wings out of rolled up newspaper, stuffed stockings or strips of crepe paper.

5. Securely attach the puppet's head, arms, wings and legs to the puppet's body with staples and masking tape.

6. Attach a string to the puppet's head and hang it around the neck so that the puppet hangs in front of the puppeteer. The puppet's head should cover the puppeteer's chest.

7. If you want, you can attach the puppet's arms and legs or wings to the puppeteer's own arms and legs with rubberbands or string, so that the puppet can walk, dance, wave or fly.

Act: The children should practice acting out the story without wearing the body puppets first, paying attention to the way the characters move and what their voices might sound like. They should stay with the basic plot but feel free to improvise action and dialogue as they go along. After they have gone through the story once or twice, they can do it with the costumes. This might be fun to perform for another class!

Evaluate: Talk about how the various characters moved and if the movements were fairly typical of each animal. They may have suggestions to improve the performance.

ESSENTIAL ELEMENT THREE:
AESTHETIC GROWTH THROUGH APPRECIATION OF THEATRICAL EVENTS

Concept: View theatrical events emphasizing
player-audience relationship and *audience etiquette*

APPLAUD!

Objective: To understand that a good audience is necessary for the actors to do their best

---

Introduce: *How many of you have ever been to a play?*
What is the difference between going to a play and going to a movie?
If none have been to a play, ask:
How many have ever been to a circus, an ice skating show, or a magic show?
How is going to those performances different from seeing the same thing on television?

The major point is that the actors are right there in the same theatre as the audience. That is what makes going to the theatre different from going to a movie or watching television. The actors know the audience is there and they want to do the very best they can to entertain the audience. The actors actually know when the audience is interested in the play and likes what they are doing. Ask the children how they think the actors know that. They know it in two ways: one, the audience is quiet and listening; two, the audience laughs at funny things that happen and they clap after the show ends.

The actors, of course, are playing characters other than themselves. They are telling a story to the audience, in the form of a play. They know they aren't *really* the characters they are pretending to be, but they are doing what the characters would do in the play. It is important for the audience to help the

85

actors by imagining that the story is really happening and that the characters are real. Both the actors and the audience need to use their imaginations, if the theatrical experience is to be a good one.

Plan and Act: Over a period of several days, give the children the experience of being both the performer and the audience. Ask them to tell a joke to the rest of the class. The audience is to imagine it is the funniest joke they have ever heard. They respond by laughing and clapping enthusiastically. You can even go so far as to have a joke told a second time by some of the children, while the audience whispers and gives no response at the end. Ask them how the audience made them feel each time.

Another way to reinforce the actor/audience relationship is to replay some of the activities done previously or plan new ones. The class is directed to show how a good audience would respond.

AUDIENCE ETIQUETTE

Objective: To know how to respond appropriately as an audience member

Introduce: First, discuss the meaning of the word "etiquette" in other situations they are familiar with, such as table manners, or being a guest in someone else's home.

There are certain things one does when going to the theatre, too, in order to be a good audience. See if they can think of some possibilities and list them on the board. Try to elicit other ideas from them by asking "What if . . ." questions to fit the rules of etiquette below. For example, "What if some people arrive late and have a hard time finding a seat. How would that affect the rest of the audience?"

Audience Etiquette

1. Arrive promptly for the scheduled performance.
2. Take care of bathroom business and drinks of water before taking your seat.
3. Be considerate of others around you. While waiting for the performance to begin, talk quietly and keep your hands, arms, and feet to yourself.
4. Just before the performance begins, usually the lights are dimmed and sometimes it is totally dark for a few seconds. Show your knowledge of this theatrical technique by sitting calmly when the lights go out.
5. Do not talk to your friends during the performance.
6. Save eating and drinking until after the performance.
7. Show respect for the actors by giving them your full attention during the performance. Show your appreciation for their work by applauding.
8. When the performance is over, wait patiently for your turn to exit.

Plan and Act: Practice entering the room and the rules of etiquette before attending a performance. Even though you may not be able to darken the room totally, turn off one bank of lights at a time to signify the dimming of the lights. Then turn on the lights for the "stage."

Some of the children may want to replay an earlier story they have done or perform one of their puppet shows. Whether they are actors or audience, the children should pretend they are at a real theatre.

Concept: View theatrical events emphasizing awareness of the following: *physical attributes and objectives of characters; dramatic conflicts; prediction of plot resolution.*

> **NOTE:** Viewing theatrical events means going to a theatre, or seeing a performance by a touring group who comes to the school. Most theatre companies will provide study guides to help prepare the children for a performance, and to further their understanding through follow-up activities.

The following lesson is based on a play, *The Fool of the World and the Flying Ship,* included here. The lesson serves as a model of how to analyze certain aspects of a play. The play can either be performed by the students for their own benefit, or simply read out loud.

THE FOOL OF THE WORLD AND THE FLYING SHIP

Objective: 1. To analyze the physical attributes and objectives of the characters.
2. To recognize dramatic conflicts.
3. To predict the resolution of the plot.

Introduce: Tell the children to try to get pictures in their mind of what the characters look like and what they are doing as they read the play.

Present: *THE FOOL OF THE WORLD AND THE FLYING SHIP*

Characters

Narrator	Listener
Father	Hopping Man
Mother	Drinker
Oldest Son	Eater
Middle Son	Wood Carrier
Fool of the World	Servant
Old Man	Tsar
	Messenger

A play in four scenes

Scene 1 At home
Scene 2 On the road
Scene 3 Flying
Scene 4 Courtyard and Palace of the Tzar

SCENE 1

NARRATOR:
In Russia, long ago, there lived a farmer and his wife who had three sons. Two of the sons were clever, handsome and charming, but the third was so quiet and did so little that he was called the Fool of the World. His parents cared a great deal for their two older sons but thought so little of the Fool that they sometimes even forgot to fix enough food for him to eat. One evening when the family was eating dinner, there was a knock on the door.

FATHER:
Who do you suppose that is?

MOTHER:
If you will go and open the door, we will find out.

FATHER: (Opens the door)
Hello, friend. How can I help you?

MESSENGER:
I am a messenger from the Tsar. Are there any young men living here?

FATHER:
Oh yes, yes. Please come in.

MESSENGER: (Enters)
The message is this: The Tsar wishes to have a flying ship — one with wings that could sail all over the sky. He will give his daughter, the princess, in marriage to anyone who can build such a ship. (Exits)

MOTHER: (Talking to the two older sons)
What a wonderful chance for you two clever boys!

OLDEST SON:
Yes, mother, it certainly is! Come, brother, let's get our things together and leave this very night.

MIDDLE SON:
Fine brother! I'm sure that one of us, at least, can build the ship *and* become a great man when he marries the Tsar's daughter.

FATHER:
Mother, get some fine food ready for them to take along while I help them pack their belongings.

NARRATOR (Mother pantomimes while the Narrator speaks)
The mother prepared cakes and pies and ripe apples and other delicious things for the sons to eat. When they were ready, she walked with them as far as the edge of town to see them safely on their way. When she returned, the Fool, her youngest son, came up to talk to her.

FOOL:
Mother, I'd like to go too. I want to make a flying ship and marry the Tsar's daughter.

MOTHER:
You! You are too stupid to go anywhere. You would be eaten by wild animals or lost before you even left our yard.

FOOL:
Oh no, I wouldn't! I want to go! I want to go!

MOTHER:
No! Now be quiet.

FOOL:
I won't be quiet, Mother. I want to go. I do, I do!

90

SCENE 2

NARRATOR: (Mother and the Fool pantomime while the Narrator speaks)
Because of the Fool's nagging, his mother finally gave in and let him go. She gave him some stale crusts of bread to eat and a bottle of water to drink. She said goodbye at the door of the house. She cared so little for the Fool, that she had forgotten all about him by the time she closed the door.

The Fool was not unhappy with the way his mother treated him because he did not know that things could be different. Besides, there was a great adventure ahead of him, and he was eager to be on his way. He sang as he walked down the road. he had not gone far, when he met an old man.

OLD MAN:
Hello, my boy.

FOOL:
Hello, Old Man.

OLD MAN:
Where are you going?

FOOL:
Oh, haven't you heard? The Tsar wants someone to build a flying ship for him, and then he will let the person who builds the ship marry the Princess. I am going to build the flying ship myself.

OLD MAN:
Do you know how to make a flying ship?

FOOL:
No, I don't.

OLD MAN:
What will you do then?

FOOL:
Heaven only knows!

OLD MAN:
Well, let's have something to eat and rest a while. Then we can talk more about this.

FOOL:
The food I have is not very good — I am really ashamed to offer it to you to eat. But you are welcome to share it.

OLD MAN:
That's all right. Open your bag. I think you might be surprised at what you'll find.

FOOL: (Opening the bag)
Why, what's this? My mother put crusts of bread and some water in my lunch but they are not there now! Here are fresh rolls, cooked meats, fruit, and a bottle of ale! Where did they come from?

OLD MAN:
Don't worry about where they have come from. Someone powerful loves you, even if your mother does not. Let's get to eating some of the good food.

NARRATOR:
The Fool and the Old Man had a wonderful time eating and laughing. They even sang some songs when they were finished. When the merry making was over, the Old Man spoke to the Fool.

OLD MAN:
Because you are kind and generous, I will tell you how to get a flying ship. Listen carefully, for you must do exactly as I say.

FOOL:
Oh, I will, I will!

OLD MAN:
Go down this road into the forest. Stop in front of the first big tree you see. Turn around three times, then hit the tree with your hatchet. Fall backward on the ground and close your eyes. You will fall asleep. When you wake up, the flying ship will be ready. You may get in the ship and fly off wherever you want to go. But be *sure* to give

a ride to everyone you meet along the way. Is all this clear to you?

FOOL:

Oh yes, oh yes! Thank you so much. I will do exactly as you say. Goodbye! Goodbye!

SCENE 3

NARRATOR: (The Fool pantomimes the action as the Narrator speaks)
The Fool did as the Old Man had told him. He stopped at the first big tree he saw and struck it sharply with his hatchet. Then he let himself fall backward to the ground and lay there with his eyes tightly shut. At once he fell sound asleep. When he awoke, there where the tree had stood was a little flying ship, complete with wings. The Fool jumped in, and off the ship sailed. The Fool sailed above the highway so he would not get lost. As he flew along above the highway, he looked down and saw a man with his ear pressed to the ground.

FOOL: (Flies close to the ground)
Hello, friend. What are you doing?

LISTENER:
Hello to you, friend. I am listening to everything being said in the world.

FOOL:
Come fly with me. I may need you.

LISTENER:
All right, I'd like to do that.

NARRATOR:
The listener got in, and he and the Fool flew on, talking and singing together. Soon they saw a man hopping on one leg while he held on to the other leg by the ankle.

FOOL:
Good morning, friend. Why are you holding on to one leg?

HOPPING MAN:
I take such big steps that if I used both legs I would step clear across the world in one stride.

FOOL:
Well, with such power as that we may need you. Come with us.

HOPPING MAN:
Thank you, I'd like to do that.

NARRATOR:
The three men flew on and on until they spied a man carrying a huge bag on his back.

FOOL:
Good day, sir. What is in your sack?

EATER:
Oh, just a thousand or two loaves of bread.

FOOL:
Where are you going?

EATER:
I'm going to get some more bread for dinner.

FOOL:
But you have so much bread in your sack already!

EATER:
Oh, that little bit? That's only enough for one mouthful.

FOOL:
My goodness! Come with us. We might need you.

EATER:
Thank you, I'd like that!

NARRATOR:
Again the ship flew on, getting ever closer to the Tsar's palace. As

they flew over a lake, the Fool saw a man walking around and around as if he were looking for something.

FOOL:
Hello, friend. Are you looking for something?

DRINKER:
Yes, I'm trying to find a drink of water.

FOOL:
Well, you have a whole lake in front of you. Why not drink from that?

DRINKER:
Oh, there is not enough water there to even wet my throat.

FOOL:
Well, I'm sure that you would fit in with our group. Come, fly with us!

DRINKER:
Fine, I'd like to do that.

NARRATOR:
They flew on and on and on. Then they saw a man with a bundle of sticks on his back, heading toward the forest.

FOOL:
Say, friend, why are you taking your bundle of sticks into the forest? The forest is already full of sticks.

WOOD CARRIER:
Oh, these are not ordinary sticks.

FOOL:
What do you mean?

CARRIER:
If I put these sticks on the ground, they will turn into a whole army of soldiers.

FOOL:
Really? Then come with us, friend. With such magic, we need you.

CARRIER:
With pleasure! This wood is heavy to carry.

SCENE 4

NARRATOR:
The Fool and his friends met no one else on the road, and before long they reached the Tsar's palace where they flew down and anchored their ship in the courtyard.

FOOL:
Well, here we are. Now the Tsar will give me his daughter in marriage.

LISTENER:
I hope you are right, friend.

SERVANT:
Here! You peasants! What are you doing in the Tsar's courtyard? Get out of here!

FOOL:
No. I have come to give the Tsar this flying ship and to marry his daughter.

SERVANT:
Marry his daughter? You must be a fool to think that. You must wait until I tell the Tsar.

NARRATOR:
The servant hurried away to tell the Tsar what the Fool had said.

TSAR:
The peasant wants to marry *my* daughter? Even if he does give me the flying ship. I can't let my daughter marry a stupid peasant, no matter what I promised. I know — I'll make him do such hard things before

he can marry my daughter, that he will never be able to do them. Then I'll have both my daughter *and* the flying ship!

SERVANT:
What a clever idea, Your Majesty!

TSAR:
Go to the fellow in the flying ship and tell him that I am thirsty and want a cup of the magic Water of Life. And I want it within an hour.

SERVANT:
I will, Your Majesty.

NARRATOR:
While the Tsar and the Servant had been talking, the Listener had his ear to the ground and heard everything they said. He told the Fool what he had heard.

FOOL:
Oh my, what shall I do? If I searched for a hundred years, I'd never find the Water of Life. And he wants it in an hour!

HOPPING MAN:
Never fear, my friend. I'll use both my legs and go get the water for you. (He lets go of his foot and runs off stage. He runs right back again, carrying a cup of water.) Here you are! The magic Water of Life!

FOOL:
Already? Thank you so much! (Gives the water to the Servant) Here is the water the Tsar wanted. Take it to him and tell him that now I want to marry his daughter. (The Servant takes the water to the Tsar).

TSAR: (Surprised)
How could these peasants have gotten the water so quickly? Well, I must think of something else impossible for them to do. I have it! Servant, go to the flying ship and tell the men there that since they are so clever, they must also be very hungry. They must eat at one meal, as much bread as one hundred ovens can bake and twelve roasted oxen.

SERVANT:
Yes, Your Majesty. I will give them your message right now.

NARRATOR:
Of course, the Listener heard what the Tsar had said and told the Fool.

FOOL:
Why, what shall I do? I can't even eat one loaf of bread at a time. I surely can't eat hundreds of loaves! And the roasted oxen!

EATER:
Don't worry. I can easily eat this little snack that the Tsar is going to give us. But I wish he'd let me have a full meal!

NARRATOR:
The Eater gobbled the bread and the oxen, bones and all, and even complained that he was still hungry! So then the Tsar decided that the fool and his friends must drink forty barrels filled with cider. The Listener told the Fool what he heard the Tsar say.

FOOL:
Why, I never drank even a quart of cider at one time. I certainly can't drink forty barrels full.

DRINKER:
Well, I can. You forget how thirsty I am. This will just be enough to wet my throat. I'll be back in a minute. (Goes off stage and comes right back, smacking his lips) I'm sorry there were only forty barrels. I'm still thirsty!

SERVANT: (Runs to the Tsar)
The cider is all gone, Sire!

TSAR: (Very angry)
All gone? Shall I never get rid of this fellow? Give him this message. If he is to marry my daughter, he must have an army of soldiers to take care of her, and he must bring the army here by tomorrow morning. That will stop him!

SERVANT:
Yes, Your Majesty!

NARRATOR:
When the Listener gave the Fool the messge, the Fool was completely discouraged.

FOOL:
Well, dear friends, I am done for. You have helped me all you can, and I appreciate it.

WOOD CARRIER:
Have you forgotten about me and my wood? I'll take care of everything. Don't worry.

FOOL:
Thank you, thank you, dear friend. When the servant comes, I'll tell him to tell the Tsar that if I can't marry the Princess tomorrow, I'll make war on this country and take her away by force.

NARRATOR:
The servant gave the Tsar the message. And during the night the wood carrier spread his sticks around, and each stick turned into twenty soldiers. The courtyard was filled with soldiers, and hundreds more stood in rows outside the castle gates.

In the morning, when the Tsar awoke, he was so frightened when he saw the soldiers with their guns and swords that he decided he had better keep his promise and not try any more tricks on so powerful a magician as the Fool. He sent a beautiful suit of clothes and rich jewels to the Fool to put on and begged him to marry the Princess.

The Fool and the Princess fell in love when they met. They were married that very day and, of course, they lived happily ever after. As for the Tsar, he spent the rest of his days flying around happily in his beautiful flying ship!

The following are questions about the characters. Some of the answers are found directly in the script. Others rely on the students' imaginations, as they picture what a particular character might be like.

Father and Mother:

How do they feel about their sons?
Why don't they love the youngest son?
What do they do that shows they don't love him?
How might their voices sound when they talk to the two oldest sons?
How might they sound when they talk to the Fool?
What is their objective with regard to the two oldest sons?
(That is, what do they want them to do?)
What is their objective with regard to the Fool?

Fool:

What is his objective? (To marry the princess.)
Why does he want to make a flying ship?
Why is he surprised when he opens his lunch bag?
How does he feel when he flies up in the air?
Is he ever worried that he might not succeed in doing all the Tsar asks him to do?
How did he show that he wasn't a fool?

Old Man:

Who was he?
What did he look like?
What was his objective?
Why did he decide to help the Fool?

Listener, Hopping Man, Eater, Drinker, Wood Carrier:

What does each character look like?
What is each doing when the Fool sees them?
Do they have anything to do with the Old Man?
What is their objective?
What do they think of the flying ship?

100

Tsar:

What does he look like?

What is his objective?

Why does he ask the Fool to do impossible tasks?

What does he think when the Fool gives him the magic Water of Life?

What does he think each time the Fool does what he was commanded to do?

Why does he finally beg the Fool to marry his daughter?

Servant:

What does he look like?

How does he walk?

What is his objective?

What does he think of the Tsar? The Fool?

Questions about the dramatic conflict:

What is the main conflict? (The Fool wants to marry the princess and the Tsar won't let him.)

Each problem that arises makes the conflict stronger.

List the various problems, or crises, in the order in which they happen.

What was the climax, the turning point, of the play? (The army and its affect on the Tsar.)

Questions about the resolution of the plot:

How was the basic conflict resolved?

When did you get the first clue about what might happen at the end?

What could have happened to change the ending? For example, what if the Fool had not picked up all of the people he saw?

What if the princess did not fall in love with the Fool?

Staging Considerations: If the class is going to act out the play, they should keep the audience in mind when they answer the following questions.

What props would be helpful to use in the play?

How can the actors use the stage so it seems as if they are flying for many miles?

*How can the Fool and his friends make it seem as if they are all flying in
the flying ship?*

*How can the acting area be used so that one part is the courtyard of the
palace and another is in the throne room of the Tsar?*

*When acting the play, be sure to keep the action and the conversation
moving quickly. There should not be pauses between speeches except
when some action takes place.*

SEEING A PLAY

Objective: To attend a live theatre production and discuss
it afterward

Before the play: Most theatre companies provide a study guide for
teachers to use with students both before and after the play. Such a guide can
help prepare the students for seeing the play. The better prepared they are,
the more they are likely to enjoy the performance. They will anticipate what is
about to happen, and know something about the plot and characters.

If the play is based on a story or book, you may want to read the story, or
excerpts from the story, to the class. They will understand the play better, if
they know the basic plot beforehand.

You might want the students to act out a few of the more exciting scenes
before they see the play. You could also ask them to recall and enact times
when they were afraid, or sad, or joyous, just like the characters in the story.
They will find it interesting to compare what they did with what the actors do
in the play.

If there are any concepts or words you think they might not understand,
these should be reviewed beforehand.

If the play is set during a particular historical period, you might want to
bring in some pictures of the period. Discuss the types of clothes people
wore, what kind of transportation they used, what kind of homes they lived in.

102

After the play: Providing a variety of ways for students to respond to seeing the play is important to reinforce their learning. If you were given a study guide, you may find follow-up suggestions that will appeal to your class. The following is a list of activities which many teachers have found useful. Obviously these are "generic" suggestions, and you would want to tailor them to fit the particular play the class saw.

1. Draw your favorite character, or the most exciting scene.
2. Draw the set.
3. Dramatize:
    a. Show how each of the characters walked.
    b. Choose one scene from the play to act out. Why was that scene selected?
    c. Act out a different ending for the play.
    d. Act out a scene from another story which shows courage, feeling afraid, reaching a goal — whatever is appropriate to the play that was seen.
4. Discuss:
    a. What was the most exciting part of the play? How did you feel during that part?
    b. Who was your favorite character? What did you like about him or her?
    c. What was the objective of each character?
    d. How was the play the same, or different, from the story or book it was based on? (If appropriate.)
    e. What was the main conflict? How was the conflict resolved?
    f. What could have happened to change the ending?
    g. How did the designers of the scenery, costumes, props and lights use their imaginations?
    h. How did you have to use your imagination when watching the play?

Concept: Recognize similarities and differences among television, film and live theatre, emphasizing *the setting and the acting.*

ACTING FOR A CAMERA

Objective: To demonstrate and discuss how acting in live theatre is different from acting in films or on television

Materials: If at all possible, use a video tape recorder, or a movie camera.

Introduce: Use the *The Fool of the World and the Flying Ship* as the basis for discussion.

> *Imagine you are seeing **The Fool of the World and the Flying Ship** on television. How might it be different from seeing the play in a theatre?*

Bring out the fact that the mobility of the camera would allow shots on location, such as a real road, a real forest and so on. Camera tricks would even make it seem as if the flying ship were airborne! The people in a television or film audience don't have to use their imaginations as much to believe that things are really happening.

> *How is acting different on television or film from in the theatre?*
>
> *Think of sitting in a theatre. How close are the actors to you?*
>
> *There is usually quite a lot of distance between the actors and the audience.*
>
> *Now think of sitting in a movie house. The **screen** may be some distance away, but how close do the actors seem?*
>
> *In the theatre, actors often need to use bigger movements and gestures, and they even need to talk louder, so that the audience will see and hear what they are doing. They also need to make sure they are facing the audience.*
>
> *In the movies actors can use small, very natural movements and the camera will see that for us. The actors can even whisper if necessary, and the microphone will pick it up.*

Plan and Act: Use Scene 2 from *The Fool of the World and the Flying Ship* for the following activity. Ask two children to act out the scene for the rest of the class, making sure that the audience can see everything they do and hear everything they say.

Use a video camera to tape the scene, if possible. Then ask them to replay the scene, making all their movements and gestures as normal as possible, and not worrying about whether everyone in class can hear them. Tape the scene, using close-up shots when desired. Then compare the way the scene was acted the first time to the second time.

Evaluate: Play the video tape and ask them what worked well and what changes they might suggest. If you are working without a camera, talk about the kind of camera shots they imagined. Then ask them to review the differences and similarities in a play that might be done on television, film and in the theatre.

106

Chapter III:
GRADE FIVE

Fifth graders, who have been participating in this theatre arts curriculum, have had experiences in *rhythmic movement, interpretive movement, sensory awareness, emotional recall, pantomime,* and *original dialogue.* Those expressive skills are applied and reinforced in the fifth grade.

Up to this point, the majority of the creative drama lessons have centered around literary selections. In the fifth grade, students will dramatize their own *original stories.* They will continue to learn about plot structure, with special emphasis on the *nature of conflict.* They will go deeper into characterization by focusing on how a character's *attitude* is revealed in behavior.

Lessons in aesthetic growth apply the concepts the students have been working on in creative drama. For example, when they *view a theatre performance* they will be able to demonstrate their understanding of *conflict* and *character attitude.* They learn how to *evaluate* and make *informed judgements* about a theatrical event. A play script is included as a *model for analysis.*

If the students have not attended a live theatre performance before, they may benefit from the lessons on audience etiquette and the player-audience relationship in Chapter Two. In fact, a review of those points would be helpful for all students.

In Grade Five *similarities and differences among television, film, and live theatre* continue to be explored. This year the two aspects discussed are the *time of action* and *special effects.*

In the event that a class had not had prior experience in classroom drama, the Cross Reference Guide included here provides a ready access to concepts and page numbers. Classes may benefit from activities described in the fourth grade before they work on the activities for the fifth grade. In any case, the teacher may wish to review some of the earlier lessons.

On the other hand, a given class may demonstrate considerable skill in a certain concept and benefit from deepening their understanding by participating in activities from Grade Six. Students enjoy repeating theatre arts activities, so "borrowing" from another grade level is perfectly acceptable. Repeating activities within the grade level is also acceptable, and, in fact, desirable, because students become more proficient with repetition.

THEATRE ARTS
Cross Reference Guide

Essential Elements	Grade Four	Pg. No.	Grade Five	Pg. No.	Grade Six	Pg. No.
Expressive use of the body and voice	Develop body awareness and spatial perception using · *rhythmic movement* · *interpretive movement* · *sensory awareness and recall* · *pantomime* · *emotional recall*	34-36 37-39 40-43 44-46 47-48	· *rhythmic movement* · *interpretive movement* · *sensory awareness and recall* · *pantomime* · *emotional recall in character*	112-113 114-117 118-121 122-123 124-125	· *rhythmic movement* · *interpretive movement* · *sensory awareness and recall* · *pantomime* · *emotional recall in character*	165-166 167-170 171-174 175-176 177-178
	Create original dialogue	49-50	Create original dialogue	126-128	Create original dialogue	179-181

Creative drama	Dramatize literary selections using
	· *pantomime*
	· *improvisation emphasizing plot structure*
	· *characterization emphasizing*
	  · *physical attributes*
	  · *character objective*
	· *original dialogue*
	· *shadow play*
	· *puppetry*
		51-56
		
		57-61
		
		62-65
		66-70
		71-74
		75-80
		81-84
			Dramatize original stories using
			· *pantomime*
			· *improvisation and original dialogue emphasizing three kinds of conflict*
			· *characterization emphasizing attitude revealed in behavior*
			· *puppetry*
				129-130
				
				131-136
				
				137-140
				141-143
					· *pantomime*
					· *improvisation emphasizing*
					  · *setting*
					  · *time*
					· *characterization emphasizing speech revealing character*
					· *situation role playing*
						182-185
						
						186-187
						188-190
						
						191-194
						195-199

Aesthetic growth through appreciation of theatrical events	View theatrical events emphasizing · *player-audience relationship* · *audience etiquette* · *analysis of physical attributes and objectives of characters* · *recognition of dramatic conflicts* · *prediction of plot resolution* Recognize similarities and differences among television, film, and live theatre emphasizing · *setting* · *acting*	85-86, 102-103 87 88-102 104-105	· *analysis of character's attitude revealed in behavior* · *recognition of kind of conflict* · *prediction of plot resolutions* · *evaluation and aesthetic judgments* · *time of action* · *special effects*	144-154 154-156 157-158	· *analysis of how speech reveals character* · *recognition of kind of conflict* · *suggestions for alternative courses of action* · *evaluation and aesthetic judgements* · *camera angles* · *position of audience*	200-210 209-212 213-214

A NOTE BEFORE BEGINNING: The sentences which are in italic are stated as if the teacher is talking directly to the children. They are either directions, questions, or sidecoaching comments. Sidecoaching means that you are observing the children and making comments while they are acting, in order to spark their imaginations, suggest new ideas, or encourage their good work.

The italicized sentences are only intended as suggestions. Each teacher has an individual style, and should tailor remarks and questions to that style, as well as to the needs of the particular class.

GETTING STARTED

Objective: To develop an initial understanding of drama, through discussion and action

Materials: A control device, such as a drum, or tambourine

Think of your favorite television program.
What is one reason you like it so well?
Ideas might be listed on the chalkboard. Although the reasons will differ, they will probably fall into categories, such as lots of action, interesting story, interesting characters. Tell them that all their ideas are part of a subject they are going to be studying in class. The subject is drama.
What are the people called who play the various characters on television? (Actors)
An actor has tools to use, just as a carpenter has tools.
What tools do you think actors use?
Bring out the idea that the basic tool of the actor is him or herself — the *body, mind, and voice.* Actors need to keep their bodies in good condition, just as carpenters must see that their tools are always ready to work. Actors often do this by using exercises or games. Tell them that in class they will be doing some of the same things actors do, in order to sharpen their minds, bodies and voices.

110

Choose one of the rhythmic movement activities from Chapters Two, Three or Four of this book to do at this point. Before you begin, introduce the start and stop device you will be using, such as a drum, or tambourine. Establish that they start an activity only when they hear the signal, and they stop all action when they hear one single loud beat.

After the activity, ask them how they think such an activity would help actors keep their tools sharp.

ESSENTIAL ELEMENT ONE:
EXPRESSIVE USE OF BODY AND VOICE

Concept: Develop body awareness and spatial perception through *rhythmic movement*

MIRRORS

Objective: To follow and imitate someone else's movement with precision

Materials: A piece of slow, flowing music, to encourage slow movements, such as "Seagulls," from *Music for Rest and Relaxation*

The students should all stand where they can see you. Tell them that you are looking into a mirror, and they are all the mirrors. What will they do when you raise your right hand? (They will raise their left hands, like a mirror image.) Make very slow, continuous movements. The object is for the mirror image to copy your movements exactly as you do them and, as much as possible, at the same time you do them. They will get the idea after a short time.

Divide the groups into pairs. One is the person looking into the mirror, the other is the mirror image. They may make any movements they wish as long as they are slow. Tell them you will walk around and when you look at them it should be difficult to know which person is the mirror and which is moving. Reverse the roles.

To extend this lesson, suggest descriptive words for the movement. For example, move powerfully, joyfully, gracefully, heavily. Students can suggest words, as well.

CONCENTRATE!

Objective: To exchange movement patterns with a partner

This activity includes several phases. Proceed only as far as the children are able to maintain their concentration. Each time they do the activity, they should be able to go farther with it.

They work in pairs. Direct them to listen while you clap a steady four beat rhythm. (Or use a drum.) They echo what you clapped.

Next, tell them that while you clap, each pair is to decide on some kind of movement which will keep time to the beat. They both move together to the beat. Clap the four beat phrase several times, pausing between each phrase. The pairs repeat their movement phrase each time.

Next, tell them that you will clap the same rhythm, but each person is to do a different movement. The partners face each other, but each does his or her own movement to the rhythm. Repeat several times.

The next time, each person is to do what his or her partner did the last time.

Finally, draw their attention to the fact that you paused at the end of every four beats. This time, each person starts out with his or her own motion for four beats. When you begin the next set of four beats, they do their partner's motion. At the next set, they change back to their own motion. They change at each new set of four beats. This takes real concentration!

Concept: Develop body awareness and spatial perception through *interpretive movement*

CAUTIOUSLY

Objective: To create an action, stimulated by the attitude of a movement

---

Tell the class they are going to find out what parts of the body can be moved without moving the rest of the body. Begin at the bottom, with the feet. As parts are named, the whole class moves that part for a moment. After many parts are moved, ask them to try to move everything at once.

Now add something else to the movement — an attitude, such as the following:

> *Move your eyes **cautiously**.*
> *Move your head and eyes cautiously.*
> *Move your arms and head and eyes cautiously.*
> *Move around the room in that cautious way.*
> *What might you be doing? Keep moving cautiously and an idea will occur to you.*

As ideas occur, listen to them. There will probably be a great variety. Have them repeat the movement with their particular idea in mind. For example, someone might have the idea of moving a package with a bomb in it. He or she moves it carefully and cautiously, then throws it or detonates it, or whatever the student decides. Another person might have the image of walking a tight rope in a circus. They could decide what they are carrying to help them balance, and what tricks they might be dong on the tightrope.

WHO ARE YOU?

Objective: To create the action of a character, stimulated by movement

Materials: Drum or tambourine

Beat a slow, quiet beat on the drum. Tell the class to listen to the beat of the drum and move the way the beat tells them. The class moves to the beat and stops when the beat stops.

Who or what might move like that?

What might the character be doing?

Move to the beat again, becoming the character you have in mind and doing what the character would do.

Use the same slow beat, but after a couple of minutes beat with very loud, sharp bangs.

Afterward ask what characters they were and what happened when the drum sounds changed.

FIRE

Objective: To use movement to interpret a raging forest fire

Materials: Drum or tambourine

For Part One, use a lively piece of music, such as "Movin'," by Hap Palmer; For Part Two, the forest fire, a good choice is "The Internal Dance," from Stravinsky's *Firebird Suite.* For the regeneration, the "Finale," from the *Firebird Suite,* helps create the mood.

Part One: Help the class warm-up by using the movement activity described below to explore the three levels of space — low (down on the floor), middle (standing, but not reaching up), and high (reaching and leaping as high as possible).

Ask the class to find places on the floor where they won't be touching anyone else. Play a piece of lively music. Every time you hit the drum, they are to change positions, but stay in the low level of space. They should be able to make five or six changes without repeating positions. Do the same thing with the middle level.

With the high level, it will be easier for them to explore the space with continuous movement, rather than stop and start changes of positions.

Then, ask them to make movements in each level of space, varying from high, to low, to middle, as they wish.

Part Two:

How many of you have ever been around a campfire?
What is special about a campfire?
Let's create a campfire right here. Gather some wood.
They build the fire, and "light" it.
Watch the fire. Describe the way the flames move.
Each of you add one piece of wood, watch that piece, and use your hands to imitate the fire as it burns your piece of wood.
Campfires are nice, but other fires may not be so nice.
What could happen if someone dropped a match in the forest?

116

How does that kind of fire move differently from the campfire?
How does it start out? How does it progress?
What does the fire want to do? (To survive it must devour and destroy.)

Ask each one to find a place on the floor and to imagine being a twig, or a clump of dry grass or something that would easily ignite. At a signal in the music, which is easily identifiable in the "Infernal Dance," each one imagines that a match has been dropped, and they ignite.

As they play, sidecoach, using some of the descriptive words they used earlier in describing the fire.

As the fire rages, suggest to them that they suddenly come to a river.

You become panicky. You try to cross, but you can't.
You look around desperately for something else to burn, but everything is gone.
Slowly, you die down.

Fade the music out, but continue to sidecoach, suggesting the devastation of the forest:

Weeks go by, months go by, even years go by, and nothing is apparent but charred earth.

At this point, play the "Finale" softly.

Underground, something is happening.
Life is beginning to stir slowly.
Imagine you are a seed of some sort which is beginning to grow underground.
Slowly push through the earth and out into the world again.

Afterward, ask them about the feelings they experienced, both as fire and as the plant. Ask how the movements were similar and different.

You may wish to replay the fire part, adding characters of animals reacting to the fire. Whether the animals escape or not is up to them. If you do this, *be sure* they understand that those playing the fire must make it *seem* as if the fire is touching the animals, but it *must not literally touch*. A few volunteers could demonstrate how this could be done.

Afterward, a discussion of fire and its consequences would be appropriate.

Concept: Develop body awareness and spatial perception through *sensory awareness and sensory recall in character*

BLIND WALK

Objective: To experience the heightening of the senses of hearing and touch

Materials: You may want to use blindfolds for this activity

Tell the class they are going to experience what it might be like to be without sight. They work in pairs; one is designated as "A" and one is "B." The "A's" will be blindfolded, or close their eyes, and be guided around the room by the "B's." "A" should hold onto the arm of "B." "B's" must be very careful with their non-sighted partners.

They explore the room. "B's" guide "A's" to touch various surfaces, to see if they can identify them. Allow a couple of minutes for exploration. Then they reverse roles.

After several experiences, you may want to make the activity more difficult. Put some obstacles around the room, like chairs, or wastebaskets. This time the guides do not touch their non-sighted partners at all. They just walk beside them and tell them how many steps to take, when to turn, when to stop, and so on. They should move very slowly.

Discuss what they experienced when they had their sense of sight taken away.

WORD CHAIN

Objective: To listen very closely and respond at the appropriate time

Materials: An index card, or piece of paper, for each student. Each card has two words on it. The second word on one card must always be the first word on another card.
For example:

First card:	bull	Second card:	forest
	forest		hole
Third card:	hole	Fourth card:	smoke
	smoke		(and so on)

The first time the game is played, you may want to prepare the cards; other times, the students might prepare cards in groups. Explanation of the game follows. You may want to use only half the class at one time.

Distribute the cards at random. You start the story. For example:

> *Once upon a time, there was a bully whose name, appropriately enough, was Bull.*

A student in the class will have a card on which the first word is "Bull." That student takes up the story, beginning with the word "Bull." If the second word is "forest," the student must end his or her part of the story with the word "forest." For example:

> *Bull decided he would go out looking for trouble one day. He found himself cutting through a dark forest.*

Another student will have a card with the word "forest" on it, and will continue the story with that word, ending with the second word on the card.

And so it continues, with the last person concluding the story. It is permissible to add a few incidental words before the first word. For example, "In the forest . . ."

MOUTH WATERING!

Objective: To recall a favorite food, and to react to someone else's favorite food

Divide the class into pairs. Designate who is "A" and who is "B." The "A's" are to think of their favorite food to eat — something that makes their mouth water just to think of it. They are to pantomime eating it in front of their partners. The "B's" are to imagine that "A's" food is something they absolutely can't stand. "A" can't understand how "B" could possibly dislike this delicious food. Maybe "A" will try to get "B" to taste a bite of it. They may talk as they play the scene.

Then the "B's" think of their favorite food, and eat it in front of their partners. But this time "A" is to imagine that he or she also loves this feed and is sorry not to have some too.

After they have played, discuss what they tasted, and whether or not their mouths watered. Was it difficult for the partners to react to the food being eaten, if they really liked or disliked the food in reality? If so, they might try to imagine how they react to a different food which they either like or dislike, and transfer that reaction to the food their partner is eating.

SMOKE

Objective: To react to smoke in the house, playing different characters

Smells may mean different things at different times. For instance, if we were sitting around a beach fire, we would hardly notice the smell of smoke. But what if you were in bed at night and woke up smelling smoke?

Ask each student to find a place on the floor and imagine they are sleeping in their own beds. Suddenly they become aware of smoke. What would they do? If there is a fire in the house, how would they escape? Maybe it is not a fire, how would they find out? Give the signal to begin the action.

Discuss their reactions to the smoke. People react in different ways — some become panicky, some are very calm and efficient about what to do.

Divide the class into groups of four. There are four characters: a young toddler, a parent, an aged grandparent, and the family dog. They are all sleeping when one of them smells smoke.

Allow a couple of minutes for them to plan their scenes, answering questions about who smells the smoke first, what that character does, how each will respond, and how, or if, they all escape.

The groups can act out their scenes simultaneously. Afterward, one or two groups might like to repeat the scene for the rest of the class.

Discuss the reactions of the various characters. Did they make it seem as if there really was a smoke filled house? Could they make it clearer?

Concept: Develop body awareness and spatial perception through *pantomime*

COOPERATIVE PANTOMIME

Objective: To pantomime an activity in pairs and in small groups

---

Ask them to think of something they do during the day that requires only one person to do it. Examples might include brushing teeth, combing hair, playing a video game. Each one pantomimes the activity for a partner.

Then the partners decide on an activity that might take two people. For example, making the bed, washing and drying dishes, one taking a picture of the other. They show their activity to another pair.

Next, the groups of four are to decide on an activity that might take four people. If you want to make the activity harder, tell them they may not choose a game to pantomime. The groups present their pantomime for the entire class.

Afterward, discuss cooperation, asking them to think of as many things as they can that require cooperation in life.

PASS THE SPACE SUBSTANCE, PLEASE

Objective: To pantomime using an object, so that all know what it is

"Space substance" is an imaginary substance. For instance, if you hold your hands as if you were holding something the size of a basketball, you could say you were holding "space substance." Obviously the size can change at any time.

You can use this activity with the whole class in a circle, or you may want to divide into two or three small circles. Tell them that you are going to give one person in each group a space substance which can become anything they want it to be. They can make it grow bigger or smaller, blow it up like a balloon, squash it down, cut it or shape it in any way they want to. The point is to make an object out of the substance and to handle it so that everyone in the group knows what it is.

You might demonstrate by shaping a flower, for example, with a stem, leaves, and petals, and then smelling it, or picking petals off it. When the group has correctly identified the object, it is passed to the next person, who reshapes it into another object.

THE LAKE

Objective: To clearly pantomime water activities

Ask the students what water sports they like best. Each person chooses one water activity, and all pantomime simultaneously.

Afterward, help them refine their pantomimes by choosing one activity at a time and sidecoaching so they pantomime clearly. For example:

How do you get into the water when you go swimming?
How does the water feel on your body?
How much of your body do you use when you swim?
What strokes do you use?
Here comes someone asking you to waterski.

123

Concept: Develop body awareness and spatial perception through *emotional recall in character*

THE MOOD CHANGES

Objective: To establish a happy mood, which then changes to a contrasting mood

---

With the class, choose a situation in which the characters are obviously in a happy mood. Examples:

Astronauts who have made a successful landing on Mars;

Explorers who have just found buried treasure;

Hikers who have successfully climbed a mountain.

They act out the scene, establishing the mood clearly.

Then ask what could happen to change the mood so they would always shudder to remember that day. Select one of their ideas. They act it out, beginning with the previous happy mood and going through what happens to change the mood.

Afterward, discuss what various characters did that showed their feelings had changed.

EXPRESSING FEELINGS

Objective: To express a character's feelings in a given situation

Materials: Prepare two sets of index cards: one set lists actions, the other lists feelings.
Examples:

ACTIONS:	FEELINGS:
bury a pet	sadness
read a letter	happiness
enter an empty cabin at night	fear
clean the house or yard	anger

Students work in groups of three. Each group selects an Action card and a Feeling card at random. They decide *who* they are and what their relationship is (family, friends, workers, and so on), and *where* the action takes place. They are working for truthful and honest expression of feelings.

After each scene is presented, the audience identifies the characters, the action, the setting, and the feeling.

Concept: *Original dialogue*

"COME HERE"

Objective: To communicate different meanings by changing the intensity, pitch and rhythm of the voice

---

Discuss how the voice can be used to communicate different ideas, even when the words are the same. How many ways can the students think of to say the words, "Come here"? Those two words could be said with a variety of intentions, such as disgust, urgency, pleading, enticement, patience, anger, joy, questioning. Experiment with different ways.

Then ask the students to do the same thing with other words. While they walk around, for instance, they say "Hello" to other students, each time in a different way. Other words or phrases can also be used, such as "Yes," "No," "Goodbye," even "Please pass the gravy."

WHISPER

Objective: To consciously move the mouth and lips to form words more clearly, and to stress beginning and ending consonants when speaking.

The point of this lesson is to provide practice in articulation. Clear articulation is necessary in speaking aloud, as well as in whispering.

Whisper a simple direction to the class, such as, "Look out the window at the bird." Do *not* emphasize articulation or speak slowly. Some of the class may understand you, but most will not. Ask why they didn't understand you. Don't they understand whispering? Repeat the direction, this time whispering clearly and slowly, stressing beginning and ending consonants. Ask them why they understood you better that time.

In pairs, each one whispers one or two things they did after school yesterday. They whisper clearly enough so that the partner can understand every word without asking to have it repeated.

Ask a student to stand up and whisper something to the class. If they do not all understand, the student should repeat. Two or three others may also want to try.

Ask what they found themselves doing differently when they were trying to whisper clearly. Tell them to think of the way they used their mouths and lips and to repeat what they said earlier to their partner. They do it the same way, only they say it out loud instead of whispering.

Divide the class into groups of four or five. Each group is to develop a scene in which it would be natural to whisper rather than talk aloud.

Examples: someone is sick;
              robbers are entering a house;
              police are laying a trap;
              children are getting a midnight snack;
              people are trying not to set off an avalanche.

The students will be able to think of their own ideas.

VOICES AND FEELINGS

Objective: To express different feelings through variation of pitch, volume, and rate of speed

Discuss how one can tell what mood another person is in by listening to his or her voice. What do adults in their family sound like when they are in a very good mood? A bad mood?

Describe the following situations. They all act simultaneously, right after you describe the situation. There is no need for planning time.

1. *You just received your report card. You made all A's. You are overjoyed, and run to tell your best friend about it. Imagine you are talking to your best friend.*

2. *Your friend is not so happy. Your friend's report card was not good. You try to cheer your friend up.*

3. *It is dark and your pet hasn't come home. You are afraid something has happened to him. You go out to call for him.*

4. *Your bike has been stolen. Talk to your friend about it.*

ESSENTIAL ELEMENT TWO: CREATIVE DRAMA

Concept: Dramatize original stories using *pantomime*

THE STOOGES

Objective: To use clear pantomime and movement to communicate a story

Materials: Old ragtime or honky tonk piano music, such as "Chinatown, My Chinatown," would provide an appropriate background for the action

---

Introduce: Ask the class if they have ever seen the Three Stooges cartoon on television. They are three characters who can never do anything right, and are constantly getting into trouble. They might be described as corny, zany, idiotic, stupid. Are there any other characters on television that are like that?

Plan: Describe the situation: *The Stooges have decided there is no reason why man can't fly like a bird. They are in the process of completing a kite-like apparatus which they are sure will fly.*

> *What kinds of things do you think might occur as they put the finishing touches on the kite?*
> *Where will they choose to fly from?*
> *Think of what might happen and what they might do as a result.*

Other situations could be used instead of, or along with, the above:

> The Stooges decide to go into the plumbing business.
> They decide to join a circus — wild animal acts, aerial acts, and so on.
> They need to leave town in a hurry in their old jalopy.
> They go on a safari.

Divide the class into groups of three. They are to plan the scene, which is to be acted in pantomime, no dialogue. While they are planning, put the music on. Remind the class that they are cartoon characters, which means that their actions are exaggerated. Allow them two or three minutes to plan.

Act: All groups can play simultaneously. Have them start by getting into a beginning pose, as if a camera had snapped a picture of them. When they are all posed, start the music as a signal to begin. If you are using a record player, you can change the speed to 16 r.p.m. midway through the playing, so everything will be acted in slow motion. Then change to a fast speed for double-time action. After they have all played, some of the groups may want to share their scene with the rest of the class.

Evaluate: *How did the characters seem cartoon-like?*
What were some examples of clear pantomime?
Could the ending of some of the scenes be improved?

Concept: Dramatize original stories using *improvisation* which reveals an understanding of *conflict in a plot*

CONFLICT CAUSED BY PEOPLE

Objective: To improvise a scene in which the major conflict stems from people having different objectives

---

Introduce: Tell the students to close their eyes and listen. Then open and close the door quietly, but with some sound, as a person might who is sneaking in. Then tiptoe across the floor. Ask the class what they heard.

Next, tell them they will hear the same sounds, but as they listen they are to picture the following:

> *who might be coming in,*
> *what room or bulding the door is opening to, and*
> *why the person is entering in such a manner.*

Repeat the sounds and discuss their ideas.

No doubt many of their ideas would make a very interesting beginning of a play. And several might indicate a conflict. Ask them how they would define conflict. A conflict is a problem which needs solving, or an obstacle that keeps someone from doing what he or she wants to. Often a conflict arises when two people have different objectives. For example, if two friends decide to go to a movie, but each one wants to see a different movie, they have a conflict.

Plan: Divide the class into groups of three. They are to develop a scene with conflict, based on the beginning discussed before — the door opening and closing and footsteps crossing the room. They need to decide

> who the characters are,
> what the conflict is,
> what happens, and
> how they will end the scene.

Act: After a few minutes of planning, each group plays simultaneously. Then, if there are groups who would like to share their scenes with the rest of the class, they may do so.

Evaluate: Ask the students to point out who the characters were, what the conflict was, and how the scene ended. Did the conflict happen because the characters had different objectives? (For example, did one want to rob a bank and the other want to guard the money?) Tell them to try to figure out the conflict in the next television program they watch.

CONFLICT CAUSED BY THE ENVIRONMENT

Objective: To improvise a scene in which the environment causes the conflict, or problem

Materials: Cards with beginning ideas on them. (Described below.)

Introduce: Tell the class that they have learned that one of the causes of conflict is people — when people want to do different things, often a conflict arises. They may have examples to share from television.

There are other causes for conflict too. Sometimes the environment causes a problem. Do they know anyone who has allergies? Allergies are caused by the environment — foods, pollen, dust, etc. Talk about why allergies are a problem, or a conflict. What other things in the environment could cause a conflict? (Fire, floods, storms, drought, tidal waves, air pollution.) The lesson today will focus on conflict that is caused by the environment.

Plan: Divide the class into groups of three or four. Each group is given a card indicating what they are doing before the conflict arises. They are to determine what the environmental conflict will be, what they will do and how they will end the scene. Examples of cards follow. It is all right if more than one group has the same card. Comparing their scenes will be interesting.

1. You are way out in the ocean in a boat, enjoying the day and fishing.
2. You are exploring a deep cave in the rocks by the beach.
3. You have been camping and you are enjoying a hike in the woods, a long way from your campsite.
4. You are enjoying a day at the beach.
5. You are shopping in a crowded mall.

Act: After they have planned their scenes, let each group act out their scene for the rest of the class. They should start by clearly establishing where they are and what they are enjoying doing before the conflict arises.

Evaluate: Following each scene, ask the class to tell what they were dong first, what the conflict was, and how the conflict changed their plans.

CONFLICT CAUSED BY ONESELF

Objective: To improvise a scene in which the conflict comes from within the character

---

This lesson has two distinct parts to it. You may choose to do the second part on a different day from the first part.

Part One:

Introduce: Tell the students to close their eyes and imagine they are in their own bed at home. Sidecoach the following:

> *Remember the way your room looks — try to recreate it in your imagination. Remember where the closet is, where various pieces of furniture are, where the door to the room is.*
>
> *Imagine that it is late at night. You and your mother are alone in the house. Other members of the family are away for a few days. The house is completely dark.*
>
> *You have wakened from a deep sleep for some reason. All of a sudden you feel very much alone. You hear the creaks in the house, but somehow they seem louder and different tonight. All sorts of ideas go through your mind. You begin to get a little scared, but you stay in your room.*
>
> *Finally you can't stand it any longer. You call out to your mother. No one answers.*
>
> *Call again. No answer.*
>
> *You are frightened. You run into your mother's bedroom. She isn't there. Now you really are frightened.*
>
> *You hear footsteps at a distance. What will you do? The steps are coming closer.*
>
> *The lights turn on. And there is your mother.*

Fear is a feeling that comes from within and it can cause a big problem or conflict if we let it. Briefly talk about times when they may have been frightened for what turns out to be no good reason. For example, going off a diving board for the first time, playing in a recital, or nightmares.

Fear is just one conflict that comes from within us. We create conflicts for ourselves in other ways as well. Have you ever wanted to do something, but you know you shouldn't? One part of you says "Do it!" The other part says, "You know you shouldn't."

Act: While they are at their desks, ask them to act out this situation.

Each of you is a boy or girl of your same age, taking a test.

The test is important because if you do well, your parents have promised to get you something you've wanted for a long time.

You are stuck on one part of the test.

You are quite sure that the person sitting next to you has the right answer, but it has always been against your principles to cheat.

Go through the process you think this boy or girl would go through.

After about 15 seconds, tell the class that when you count to five, the test papers will be collected. This is their last chance. What will they do?

Evaluate: Be open and receptive to students' individual opinions. Talk about how cheating on a test is not acceptable behavior and will hurt the student in the long run.

Part Two:

Introduce: Sometimes our mouths get us into trouble or conflict.

Have you ever said something and then immediately were sorry you said it?

Sometimes we become so angry that we say or do things we are sorry for. Or sometimes we just don't think of the other person's feelings when we say or do something. Often we can do something to make up for our actions. But other times, nothing we say or do seems to help and only time will heal wounded feelings.

135

Plan: Divide the class into groups of two or three. They are to create a scene in which one or all in the group feel inner conflict of some sort. List some titles on the board that may help them think of an idea. Examples:

1. "I dare you!"
2. "Do you still have to do everything your parents say?"
3. "There's no such word as 'can't'."
4. "How was I to know?"
5. "It's too dark."
6. "You're just too dumb."
7. "Mama's little helper."
8. "Why did you tell?"

Allow a few minutes for them to plan their scenes. They need to figure out a good beginning and ending for the scene.

Act: Groups may volunteer to show their scenes to the rest of the class.

Evaluate: If you find that it is hard for them to act out the scenes seriously, or with good concentration, it is probably due to embarassment at expressing deep rooted feelings. Focus discussion on the content of the idea, rather than how they acted it out. Recognize that this sort of thing is difficult to do, but encourage them to do their best, just like the actors on television do.

ATTACHMENT

Objective: To reveal the attitude of a character through action and dialogue

Materials: A "costume box," with various miscellaneous items of wearing apparel, including hats, jewelry, and accessories. The students may want to contribute to the box, or you may find many items at garage sales for very low cost. The costume box can be used for many lessons.

Introduce: Each student is to choose one item to wear. After they have put it on, they find a place to stand or sit and listen while you guide their thinking. Each person answers the questions silently.

Think of a character who might be wearing what you have on.
Are you old or young?
What do you do — do you work?
Do you have a family?
What kind of house do you live in?
How do you feel — are you grumpy, cheerful, kind, mean, sad?

For some reason, you are very attached to the article of apparel you put on. You are so attached to it that you never want to take it off. You are always making excuses for leaving it on. Think of why you are so attached to it.

Plan: Ask them to find a partner, and then describe this situation for them:

The two of you have just met. You are at a party talking to each other. As you talk, each of you notices the piece of costume that the other has on and you become fascinated with it. You try very hard to get the person to take it off. You may use any method you like to get the person to take off the article in question, except physically forcing it off. What will the reaction be?
What will your reaction be when your partner wants you to remove the article you are so attached to?

139

What excuses will you invent?
Keep in mind who you are and your attitude toward the costume piece, as well as your attitude toward the other person.

Act: There is no need for the partners to plan ahead. Everyone acts simultaneously when you give the signal to begin. After they have played awhile, tell them they have one minute to end the scene in some way.

Evaluate: Discuss what they did.
What was your partner's attitude toward the piece of clothing?
How could you tell?
What were some of the excuses your partner invented?
How did you end the scene?

Concept: Dramatize original stories using *puppetry*

THE ADVENTURES OF . . .

Objective: To construct sock puppets, invent a plot, and act out a play

Materials: Socks;
Lightweight cardboard, or 3″x5″ index cards;
Material for stuffing the head — cotton, old stockings, etc.;
Fabric remnants, handkerchiefs, bandanas;
Yarn, buttons, felt scraps, various kinds of trim;
Scissors, needle and thread, glue, rubberbands, masking tape

Introduce: Ask the class what an adventure is. Solicit ideas for what they think would be good adventures. Then tell them that they may be able to go on some of those adventures — except it won't happen to them, it will happen to the puppets they create.

They are each to think of a character they would like to create. Maybe it is Detective Dog, or Cranky Crocodile, or Grim Granny, or Fabulous Felicia. The character can be an animal or a person. They can be thinking of the character they want to make while they construct the basic puppet figure. After that, they will add the features and costumes which will give the puppet its own unique personality.

CONSTRUCT:

1. Make a tube of cardboard, about 5 inches long and wide enough to fit the index finger. Put the tube into the toe of the sock.

2. Stuff the toe of the sock with cotton or old stockings. This will become the head of the puppet.

3. Tie a string around the base of the head, around the tube to create the neck.

4. Cut slits in the side of the sock for the thumb and third finger.

5. Make a simple basic costume:

Cut a hole in the center of a bandana size piece of material.

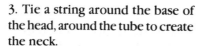

Pull the bottom of the sock through the hole and tie it with thread or a rubberband around the neck.

Put the puppet on and gather the material around the thumb and middle finger (the puppet's arms) and secure with a rubberband. The puppet is now basically ready to perform — it just needs a personality!

6. Sew or glue features on. Add yarn or other material for hair. Add anything else to the basic costume that will help it come "alive."

142

Plan: Divide the class into groups of three or four. They should discuss their puppets and devise an adventure for the characters. Remind them that a plot has a beginning, middle and end, that there should be a strong conflict of some sort which builds to a climax before the end. They should write down the order of the action they plan.

If there are any props needed for their puppets, they should gather them together or construct them. Do they want sound effects? Those can be tape-recorded.

The stage can be as simple as a table top which they kneel behind. The front should be draped with material or paper to conceal the puppeteers in back.

Act: Each group should rehearse several times before presenting their puppet adventure for the class. Even these simple puppets are capable of a variety of movements. It is important that there is movement on stage — the puppets don't just appear and "talk," without using appropriate head and arm gestures. Ask them to think about puppets they have seen on television and how they move.

Evaluate: Afterward, talk about their adventures, and especially the plot structure.

> *Was the action of the story clear?*
> *What was the conflict?*
> *What was the climax?*
> *Could the play have been improved?*

These puppets can be used in a variety of ways and in many combinations for future puppet plays.

ESSENTIAL ELEMENT THREE:
AESTHETIC GROWTH THROUGH THE APPRECIATION
OF THEATRICAL EVENTS

Concept: View theatrical events emphasizing
analysis of character attitude revealed in behavior;
recognition of kind of conflict;
prediction of plot resolution;
evaluation and aesthetic judgments

> **NOTE:** Viewing theatrical events means going to a theatre, or seeing a performance by a touring group who comes to the school. Most theatre companies will provide study guides to help prepare the children for a performance, and to further their understanding through follow-up activities.

The following lesson is based on a play, *The Squire's Bride,* included here. The lesson serves as a model of how to analyze certain aspects of a play. The play can either be performed by the children, or simply read out loud.

THE SQUIRE'S BRIDE

Objective:
1. To analyze the characters' attitudes as they are revealed in behavior
2. To recognize the kind of conflict represented in the play
3. To predict the resolution of the plot
4. To evaluate and make aesthetic judgments

Introduce: Ask the class to give examples of times when someone has insisted they do something they really didn't want to do. How does that make them feel?

The play they are about to read deals with that kind of situation and the clever solution that was found. Tell the children to picture the characters, as they read, and how they look when they respond to what happens.

Present: *THE SQUIRE'S BRIDE*

Characters

Squire	Jim
Mary Jones	Ned
Farmer Jones,	Wedding guests
Mary's father	(8 to 10)
Horse	Narrator

A play in four scenes.
Scene 1   The farm
Scene 2   Later, on the farm
Scene 3   The Squire's house
Scene 4   Living room of the Squire's house

SCENE 1

NARRATOR:
There was once a very rich Squire, who had everything he could buy with money, but he was not happy because he was lonely. He had a wife at one time but she died, so the Squire decided to look for another bride. One day when he was out in his yard, he saw Mary Jones, the daughter of the farmer who lived next door, working in the field. She was pretty and very strong and the Squire thought she would make a good wife. He knew her family was poor, and so he was sure that Mary would want to marry a rich man like himself! The fact that the Squire was fat, bald, and much older than Mary didn't seem to bother him at all. He was sure that his money would be all any girl could want. So the Squire crossed the field to where Mary was working and began to talk to her.

SQUIRE:
Hello, Mary. Fine day, isn't it?

MARY: (Keeps on hoeing the field)
Hello, Squire. Yes, it is.

SQUIRE: (Sighing)
It's hard to feel sad on such a beautiful day, but I do.

145

MARY: (Keeps working and doesn't look up)
Oh really?

SQUIRE:
Yes, I've been lonely since my wife died last year. In fact, I think it's time that I married again.

MARY:
Maybe some nice, older lady will want to marry you.

SQUIRE:
Oh, I wasn't thinking of an *older* lady. In fact, I was thinking of you!

MARY:
Me? Oh, no thank you. I don't want to marry you.

SQUIRE:
Mary, don't be silly. I have so much money you would never have to do hard work again as you are doing now. Of course you want to marry me!

MARY:
But I like to work outdoors. And even if I didn't, I would not marry you!

SQUIRE:
You know, Mary, you are being foolish. Very few girls have the chance to marry a man as important and rich as I am.

MARY:
Well, I'm sure you'll find someone who cares for your money as much as you do, but it's not me! Goodbye! (Leaves the stage)

SQUIRE:
Mary! Mary! Come back!

FARMER JONES: (Enters)
Hello, Squire. Is something wrong?

146

SQUIRE:
Yes, there is, to be sure. I have done your daughter the great honor of asking her to be my bride and she refused!

FARMER JONES:
Refused? So fine a gentleman as you? I don't understand.

SQUIRE:
Neither do I, Farmer Jones. I think maybe she is just too young to know what is good for her. As her father, maybe you should make the decisions for her. In fact, I will make a bargain with you. When you convince her to marry me, I will cancel the debt of money that you owe me, and I will give you that piece of land you wanted, down in the meadow.

FARMER JONES:
Well, that's mighty generous of you. You just leave things to me. I'll bring Mary to her senses. She doesn't know what's good for her.

SQUIRE:
It's nice to deal with a reasonable man. I'll be going home now. I think you should talk to her right away.

FARMER JONES: (While Squire exits)
Oh yes, I certainly will. Just leave everything to me. I'll convince Mary!
Mary! Mary! Come here, please.

MARY: (Enters)
Did you want me, Father?

FARMER JONES:
Yes, I did, child. What's this I hear about you not wanting to marry the Squire?

MARY:
I don't want to marry that old goat. I not only don't want to marry him, I'm not going to marry him!

FARMER JONES:
Now, daughter, he is a rich man and if you marry him, we'd never have to worry about money again.

MARY:
I don't care how rich he is. I wouldn't have him if he sat buried up to his neck in gold!

FARMER JONES: (Sternly)
Mary, as your father, I order you to marry the Squire!

MARY:
And as your daughter, I refuse! (Leaves stage)

FARMER JONES:
Come back here, Mary! Mary! Oh my, that girl has a mind of her own, just like her mother. What shall I do now? The Squire wants an answer right away and I can't tell him she said no! Oh my.

SCENE 2

NARRATOR:
The farmer stayed away from the Squire for several days, but finally the Squire insisted on knowing what Mary would do. The only plan the farmer could think of was this: First, the Squire was to get everything ready for the wedding, and then the Squire was to send for Mary as if he wanted her to do some work for him. When she arrived, they would be married so quickly, she would not have time to think about it. The Squire agreed to the plan and went home to prepare for the wedding. He invited his guests, and when everyone had arrived he sent two of his servants to the farmer's house. They were to say to the farmer, "We have come for what you promised the Squire."

JIM:
Well, Ned, here's the farm. Where's the farmer?

NED:
I don't know. Farmer Jones! Farmer Jones!

MARY: (Enters)
Hello, did you want something? I'm Mary Jones. My father's not here.

JIM:
Oh. Well, the Squire is in a big hurry to have your father send him what he promised him.

MARY:
A hurry? Why?

NED:
Oh, he's having a big party! And those were his instructions.

MARY:
Oh, I see! (To herself) **I've been wondering what father and the Squire were up to! I think I'm beginning to understand.** (To Ned and Jim) **Oh yes, now I remember. What you want is that little horse of ours, over in the field. Better go and get her. It isn't right to keep the Squire waiting.**

JIM:
All right. Thank you. Come on, Ned.
(Both go up to the horse and led her back to the Squire's house while the Narrator speaks.)

SCENE 3

NARRATOR:
Now, audience, we ask you to imagine that this is a real horse. She doesn't speak but, as you may know, she is very important to our play. The boys took the horse back to the Squire's house. They left the horse in front of the house and went in to report to the Squire.

SQUIRE:
Well, did you get her?

NED:
Oh yes, sir. She's outside.

SQUIRE:
Well, while I take care of my guests, you take her to the room my mother had.

JIM: (Bewildered)
But how can we do that, Master?

SQUIRE:
You'll have to figure that out. Get some more people to help, if you can't manage her alone. (Leaves the room)

JIM: (Jim and Ned go off stage and return pulling and shoving the horse.)
Come on, Ned. Push harder!

NED:
Are you sure Squire wants this horse in the bedroom? Seems crazy to me!

JIM:
Me too. But that's what he said.
(Both struggle with the horse, who does not want to go with them. Finally, they get her in the bedroom.)

(Squire and Jim both go into the livingroom from different directions at about the same time.

JIM: (Hot and panting)
Well, Squire, we did it! It was the hardest job we've ever had to do around here.

SQUIRE:
Never mind. There was a good reason for it. Now send a maid to help her dress in the wedding clothes on the bed.

JIM:
Dress? But Master . . .

SQUIRE:
No back talk! Tell the maid not to forget the veil and wreath.

JIM:
Yes sir.

(Squire exits.)

SCENE 4

NARRATOR:
Jim told a maid in the kitchen to go upstairs and dress the horse in the wedding clothes, so she would look like a bride. Jim and the others thought the Squire was playing a joke on his friends. So the woman laughed and did as she was told. In the meantime, the Squire brought his guests into the living room.

SQUIRE: (Entering with guests)
Good friends, as you no doubt have guessed, we are about to have a wedding in this house. The bride has been feeling a little shy about being a part of all this splendor, but I told her you were all good friends of mine and she was not to worry.

JIM: (Enters and interrupts the Squire, whispering to him.)
She's ready.
(He goes out, giggling. The guests whisper excitedly among themselves, wondering who the bride is.)

SQUIRE: (Proudly)
Quiet, everyone! Here comes my bride!
(He majestically turns away toward the audience, so that he doesn't see the horse enter. The guests do see the horse and they begin to giggle. Jim and Ned are pushing the horse, who clatters into the living room.)

SQUIRE: (Still facing away, but putting his arm out to the side.)
Mary, my beautiful bride, come here by me.
(He is smiling and turns to greet his bride. His smile freezes on his face as his eyes grow wide with astonishment. He laughs feebly and falls over in a faint.)

NARRATOR:
The guests laughed about that wedding for months, and as for the Squire, he never went looking for a bride again!

Discuss the characters: The following questions can be used to help the class plan how they will perform the play, or just to discuss after they have read the play. Some of the answers are found directly in the script. Others rely on the students' imaginations, as they picture what a particular character might be like.

Mary Jones:

In the opening of the play, how does Mary behave that lets you know how she feels about the Squire?

Why doesn't she want to marry him?

What does she think about her father?

How do you know she has a sense of humor?

Squire:

What does he look like?

Based on what he does and says, what kind of a person is he?

Why does he keep insisting that Mary will marry him?

What is his attitude toward Mary?

How does he behave when he is with her?

What is his attitude toward Jim and Ned?

How does it happen that he doesn't find out that the bride is a horse until the very end?

Farmer Jones:

Why is he so anxious to have his daughter marry the Squire?

How does this show when he talks with Mary?

Do you think Mary often does what he tells her to?

How does he feel when she refuses to marry the Squire?

Jim and Ned:

What is their attitude toward the Squire?

What do they think when the Squire tells them to take the horse to the bedroom?

What does Jim think when the Squire tells him the horse is to be dressed like a bride?

Wedding Guests:
> How do they feel about the Squire?
> Why did they want to attend the wedding?
> What do they think when the "bride" comes in?
> How do you think they reacted?

The "Bride":
> Assuming two people are playing the horse, what do you think the attitude of the horse is to all that is happening?

How might the horse move that would show how she felt?

Discuss the conflict and plot resolution:
> Based on knowledge of the three kinds of conflict, what kind of conflict does this play represent — person against person, person against environment, or person against himself?
>
> What is the Squire's objective? How does that put him in conflict with Mary? How does Farmer Jones contribute to the conflict?
>
> What is the high point, or climax, of the play?
>
> At what point in the play did you get the first clue about what might happen? (When she sends the horse)
>
> What was the second clue? (When the horse is to be dressed as a bride.)
>
> What makes it funny? (Our sympathies are with Mary — no one likes to be forced into doing something, especially something so important as marriage. The play is funny because the audience is aware of what is happening, but the Squire is totally unaware until the very end. The audience enjoys the trick played on him.)

Stage Considerations: Even if the students are not performing the play, they can discuss the staging. They should keep the audience in mind when solving the following problems:
> *How will you "create" the horse? What can be used to costume the horse?*
>
> *The bedroom, where the horse is dressed, can be off stage. But the horse should be pushed and pulled into the living room, on stage,*

153

and then out through the door into the bedroom. Decide where the doors should be.

Be sure that the Squire is never in a place where he would be able to see the horse, until the very end. Plan out exactly where everyone will stand, or sit.

Evaluating and making aesthetic judgments: Since a theatrical event is a thing witnessed, not just read, one must see a performance in order to judge it. If the class has actually performed *The Squire's Bride,* you can evaluate it. If not, talk about a television show or movie most of them have seen. Questions such as the following can be tailored to most shows:

1. What did you like about it?
2. Were the characters believable within the context of the plot? Were their objectives clear? Did you know how they felt about what was happening at any given time?
3. Did the conflict and tension build through the play until the climax was reached?
4. How did the costumes help you know what the characters were like?
5. How did the scenery help you know where the action was taking place?
6. What might be done differently to improve the play?

SEEING A PLAY

Objective: To attend a live theatre production and discuss
it afterward

Before the play: Most theatre companies provide a study guide for teachers to use with students both before and after the play. Such a guide can help prepare the students for seeing the play. The better prepared they are, the more likely they are to enjoy the performance. They will anticipate what is about to happen, and know something about the plot and characters.

If the play is based on a story or book, you may want to read the story, or excerpts from the story, to the class. They will understand the play better, if they know the basic plot beforehand.

You might want the students to act out a few of the more exciting scenes before they see the play. You could also ask them to recall and enact times when they were afraid, or sad, or joyous, just like the characters in the story. They will find it interesting to compare what they did with what the actors do in the play.

If there are any concepts or words you think they might not understand, these should be reviewed beforehand.

If the play is set during a particular historical period, you might want to bring in some pictures of the period. Discuss the types of clothes people wore, what kind of transportation they used, what kind of homes they lived in.

After the Play: Providing a variety of ways for students to respond to seeing the play is important to reinforce their learning. If you were given a study guide, you may find follow-up suggestions that will appeal to your class. The following is a list of activities which many teachers have found useful. Obviously these are "generic" suggestions, and you would want to tailor them to fit the particular play the class saw.

1. Draw your favorite character, or the most exciting scene.
2. Draw the set.

3. Dramatize:
   a. Show how each of the characters walked.
   b. Choose one scene from the play to act out. Why was that scene selected?
   c. Act out a different ending for the play.
   d. Act out a scene from another story which shows courage, feeling afraid, reaching a goal — whatever is appropriate to the play that was seen.
4. Discuss:
   a. What was the most exciting part of the play? How did you feeling during that part?
   b. Who was your favorite character? What did you like about him or her?
   c. What was the objective of each character?
   d. Select three words to describe each of the characters in the play.
   e. How was the play the same, or different, from the story or book it was based on? (If appropriate.)
   f. What was the main conflict? How was the conflict resolved?
   g. What could have happened to change the ending?
   h. How did the designers of the scenery, costumes, props and lights use their imaginations?
   i. When you think about the production you saw, which colors come to mind?

Concept: Recognize similarities and differences among television, film and live theatre, emphasizing the *time* of action and *special effects*

THE SAME, BUT DIFFERENT

Objective: To recognize similarities and differences among television, film and live theatre, emphasizing time of action and *special effects*

Discuss: Ask the class to imagine they had seen *The Squire's Bride* on television. How might it be the same? How might it be different? Discuss their answers.

> *There are four scenes in the play.*
>
> *When does each scene take place? How do you know in the play version that Scene 2 takes place several days after Scene 1? The Narrator says so. If you saw it on television, there would probably not be a narrator. (Not all plays have Narrators, but this one did.)*
>
> *On television, how might you know that the time of the action was different, without a narrator? In television, a play is not filmed as one continuous play, going from the beginning to the end.*
>
> *Many different scenes can be filmed and then edited to give a sense of the passage of time. For example, we might see the conversation between the Squire and Farmer Jones making their plan. Then we might see the Squire and others making preparations for the wedding and the final wedding day results.*
>
> *There would also be time for costume changes, which would indicate passage of time.*
>
> *Tell the class to be aware of how the passage of time is handled in the next television show they watch.*

There are few special effects necessary for *The Squire's Bride*, although on television one would probably see a real horse being dressed in wedding finery, instead of people pretending to be a horse. But television and film can

157

use a much wider variety of special effects than can be used on a stage. For example, if the script calls for someone to catch on fire, that can be done on television, but would be difficult, if not impossible to do on stage. For one thing, the actor puts on a special costume. The camera shoots the burning for only a few seconds and there is a whole team of people on the set with fire extinguishing equipment.

Ask the class to think of other special effects on television or in the movies. Science fiction films provide good examples.

If possible, show the class a film, such as *The Making of E.T.* or *The Making of Star Wars*.

Although the plots may be the same on film as they are on the stage, going to the theatre requires more from the audience. The audience members need to use their imaginations more when seeing a play in a theatre. Ask the class why this is so.

160

Chapter IV:
GRADE SIX

Sixth graders, who have been participating in the theatre arts curriculum, have had experiences in *rhythmic movement, interpretive movement, sensory awareness, emotional recall, pantomime,* and *original dialogue.* Those expressive skills are applied and reinforced in the sixth grade.

Students will continue to develop their original stories for dramatization. Up to this point they have learned about plot structure and the nature of conflict. This year, they will learn how the *setting* and the *time of action* affect the plot. With regard to characterization, they have learned about physical attributes, objectives, and attitudes. This year their work will focus on how *speech* reveals a character. They will also participate in activities which stress *role playing in situations* which are of current interest and concern to the students. They will have the opportunity to understand their own and *others' points of view* by playing out scenes from several vantage points.

When they *view theatrical events,* the students will have the chance to see how the play and the acting reflect the concepts they have been learning about in their other theatre arts lessons. They will learn how to *evaluate* and make *informed aesthetic judgements.* A play script is included as a *model for analysis.*

If the students have not attended a live theatre performance before, they may benefit from the lessons on audience etiquette and the player-audience relationship in Chapter Two. In fact, a review of those points would be helpful for all students.

In the sixth grade, the students continue to explore the *similarities and differences among television, film, and live theatre.* This year the emphasis is on *camera angles* and the *position of the audience.*

In the event that a class had not had prior experience in classroom drama, the Cross Reference guide included here provides a ready access to concepts and page numbers. Classes may benefit from activities described in the fifth grade before they work on the activities for the sixth grade. In any case, the teacher may wish to review some of the earlier lessons.

THEATRE ARTS
Cross Reference Guide

Essential Elements	Grade Five	Pg. No.	Grade Six	Pg. No.
Expressive use of the body and voice	Develop body awareness and spatial perception using			
	· rhythmic movement	112-113	· rhythmic movement	165-166
	· interpretive movement	114-117	· interpretive movement	167-170
	· sensory awareness and recall	118-121	· sensory awareness and recall	171-174
	· pantomime	122-123	· pantomime	175-176
	· emotional recall in character	124-125	· emotional recall in character	177-178
	Create original dialogue	126-128	Create original dialogue	179-181
Creative drama	Dramatize original stories using			
	· pantomime	129-130	· pantomime	182-185
	· improvisation and original dialogue emphasizing three kinds of conflict	131-136	· improvisation emphasizing · setting · time	186-187 188-190
	· characterization emphasizing attitude revealed in behavior	137-140	· characterization emphasizing speech revealing character	191-194
	· puppetry	141-143	· situation role playing	195-199
Aesthetic growth through appreciation of theatrical events	View theatrical events emphasizing			
	· analysis of character's attitude revealed in behavior	144-154	· analysis of how speech reveals character	200-210
	· recognition of kind of conflict		· recognition of kind of conflict	
	· prediction of plot resolutions		· suggestions for alternative courses of action	
	· evaluation and aesthetic judgments	154-156	· evaluation and aesthetic judgements	209-212
	Recognize similarities and differences among television, film, and live theatre emphasizing			
	· time of action	157-158	· camera angles	213-214
	· special effects		· position of audience	

A NOTE BEFORE BEGINNING: The sentences which are in italic are stated as if the teacher is talking directly to the children. They are either directions, questions, or sidecoaching comments. Sidecoaching means that you are observing the children and making comments while they are acting, in order to spark their imaginations, suggest new ideas, or encourage their good work.

The italicized sentences are only intended as suggestions. Each teacher has an individual style, and should tailor remarks and questions to that style, as well as to the needs of the particular class.

GETTING STARTED

Objective: To develop an initial understanding of drama, through discussion and action

Materials: A control device, such as a drum, or tambourine

Structure the discussion around a television show the students are all likely to be familiar with and like. Ask why they like the show.

> *One reason we like certain shows is that we believe for the moment that what is going on is actually happening, even though we know the people are really actors, who go home from work just like everyone else.*

> *For example, when you see a fight on television, what makes it seem so believable? It isn't just that they have a little capsule of fake blood that releases on impact. It is all based on action and reaction, and, of course, very careful planning of each move (called choreography). If (name student in class) went over to (another student) and pretended to hit him in the stomach and (2nd student) just stood there, we wouldn't believe he had been hit at all.*

> *What would (2nd student) have to do to make it believable? He would have to double up in some way, reacting to the action of the imagined punch.*

> *As soon as I give you the signal, imagine you have been punched in the stomach.*

This would be an appropriate time to establish the use of the drum or tambourine as a start and stop signal, as well as a signal for them to freeze their positions.

> *Try it again. Remember if you are really hit, your face reacts as well as your body. Imagine you are really being hit, when I give you the signal.*
>
> *Drama is just like life, in that it is a constant series of actions and reactions.*
>
> *Imagine you have come home from school and you smell your favorite cookies. How would you react?*

Give them a series of suggestions to react to, using the start and stop signal each time. All the students can play simultaneously. They are to physically react, not just talk about what they would do. You may use the following ideas or some of your own:

> *You are walking down the street, and you sense that a stranger is following you.*
>
> *You are walking down the street when you see a hundred dollar bill.*
>
> *You are walking in the rain and you see a bedraggled little kitten who seems to be lost.*
>
> *You are walking down the street when a huge thunderstorm starts.*

Ask them which situations seemed most real to them and why. Stress the use of imagination and concentration on what is happening.

ESSENTIAL ELEMENT ONE:
EXPRESSIVE USE OF BODY AND VOICE

Concept: Develop body awareness and spatial perception through *rhythmic movement*

MIRROR RELAY

Objective: To observe closely and follow exactly

You may want to begin with the basic mirror exercise on page 112. Then increase the difficulty by directing the partners to do delayed mirrors. That is, the partner who is the mirror image waits for two or four beats before beginning the movement. The movement is continuous, but delayed just a bit. When they have mastered the delayed mirrors, they will be ready for the relay.

Ask the class to form a circle. (If you are going to play with them, join the circle. If not, stay outside the circle.) Each person looks to the left and remembers who that person is. Then they scatter throughout the room and find a place to stand, making sure they can see the person they were to remember. They do not have to be close.

Choose one person to start the movement. The person looking at the leader begins a delayed mirror — soon the whole class will be involved. After awhile tell the leader to make one last movement and freeze in position. This is a fascinating activity to watch and the students will feel like they have created an interesting piece of choreography.

BACK AND FORTH

Objective: To focus concentration on controlled movement

Sidecoach:

> *Move your arms in a gentle, swaying, swinging rhythm. Add the rest of your body, using large, swinging movements. Think of a word that might fit your rhythm. Whisper the word and fit it to the rhythm. Keep whispering it. Now say it out loud — louder, and louder.*

> *Now move in a jerky rhythm. Start with your arms and then add the rest of your body.*

> *Think of a word that fits that rhythm. Whisper it. Now say it out loud — louder, and louder.*

> *Now switch back and forth. Start with the gentle swaying rhythm. When the signal is given, switch to the jerky rhythm. Back and forth.*

To create some tension, allow less and less time between the switches.

Concept: Develop body awareness and spatial perception through *interpretive movement*

OPEN AND CLOSE

Objective: To develop a character by letting the quality of movement reveal the character.

Ask students to open and close their hands rhythmically. Explore other parts of the body that can open and close. Work up to the point where the entire body is closed, including the face, and then the entire body is open. Inhale when open, exhale when closed. End with the entire body closed, but in a standing position. Ask them to move around, maintaining the closed position.

While they are moving, sidecoach:

> *Think about what kind of person might be closed like that.*
> *What might he or she be doing?*
> *What kind of mood is the person in? Why is he or she in that mood?*
> *As you move around, say "Hello" to other people you pass as you think this person would.*

Afterward, ask them to tell something about the characters they were.

Repeat the last part of the open and closed movements again. This time end with a very open position and ask them to move around in that position. Do the same sidecoaching as before.

Afterward:

> *How were the characters in the open posture different from those with the closed posture?*
> *How did they feel toward the world and other people?*
> *Have you ever felt particularly closed or open before?*
> *How does posture reflect a person's mood or attitude?*

```
┌─────────────────────────────────────────────────────────────────┐
│                                                                   │
│   COLOR                                                           │
│                                                                   │
│   Objective: To interpret color through movement                 │
│   Materials: Colored paper or fabric                             │
│               Spotlights or slide projector                       │
│               Colored gelatins for lights                         │
│                                                                   │
└─────────────────────────────────────────────────────────────────┘
```

There are four parts to this lesson. You might want to do the first two parts on one day, and the last two or another day.

Part One: Warm-up

Ask them to stand where they have plenty of space. Sidecoach:

You have all this space around you. In a way, this space is like a blank piece of paper. On a piece of paper you could make patterns by using paints or crayons.

You can also make patterns in space by moving your bodies in various ways. See if you can move your body so it makes a curved pattern in your space. It is almost like using your whole self to fingerpaint. Make the curved pattern move. (You can use a smooth but swinging piece of music here, if you wish.)

Now use your bodies to make a pattern that is full of moving angles — all corners and sharp edges. (Fast, percussive music could be used here.) *Now try a twisted pattern. Remember there are different levels in space: very low, very high, and in-between. Fill all the levels with the moving, twisting patterns. And relax.*

Part Two: Experiencing and interpreting color by observing it.

Show them a piece of bright red paper or fabric.

The reason we see colors is because of light. Light is not stationary; it moves very fast. Some colors seem to move and vibrate. If the red you are looking at now could show us how it is moving, how might it move? What kind of pattern in space would it like to make to express its "redness"?

Find your own place in space — a place where you have enough room to work without touching anyone else. Close your eyes, and at the signal begin to move in the pattern you think red would make. The reason for closing your eyes is that right now you each have your own idea, which may be very different from somebody else's idea. Each idea is right because it is the way you think about this particular color. If your eyes are closed, you will be able to create the color movement you are thinking about, without being influenced by someone else.

While you move in your own space, say the word "red" in a way that fits your pattern — it could be long and drawn out, or it could be repeated fast and loud. It could be on one note or on many notes.

Discuss their interpretations. If they wish, half could do the red movement again, while the other half watches to see what different aspects of the color seem to come across in the movement. Then reverse players and audience.

Repeat the process with at least one other color, such as green or blue.

Part Three: Experiencing and interpreting color by being in the color.

This part of the lesson holds high appeal for students. The experience of being *in* a color is quite different from observing the color on paper or fabric. If at all possible, try to get the equipment necessary. The point is to bathe the playing area in intense color.

You can paint blank slides very intense colors — one color per slide — and use one or two slide-projectors. Or you can use two spotlights with high intensity colored gels in them. If your school does not have lighting equipment, the spotlights can be made by inserting a strong light into a two-pound coffee can. Colored gelatins — a cellophane type of material — are placed over the opening. You may have some students who would be interested in making them for class use. For this activity, each light should have the same color gel on it. The lights should be placed in front of the playing area.

Turn out all lights except the red spotlights. Ask the students to sit quietly, observing the space around them and feeling the color. Suggest that as they feel the color, it will cause them to want to move in some way or to do some activity. Give them a few moments to think, then give the signal to begin. If some students have trouble coming up with an idea, either realistic or abstract, suggest that they just begin moving and an idea is likely to occur to them.

After they play for a while, turn the regular lights on and discuss how the color made them feel. Repeat with a different color.

Part Four: Group interpretations of colors.

Divide the class into groups of four or five. Assign a color to each group, or allow them to choose their own color. It won't matter if more than one group has a certain color, since interpretations are bound to vary. Each group interprets their color in any any they wish. For example, they could choose one aspect of the color, such as fire for red, and work out a scene around fire. Or each person in the group could do something different that might be illustrative of the color.

After the groups play, evaluate by discussing what they did that communicated the color. You may want the class to follow-up by writing poems about color. (See *Hailstones and Halibut Bones,* by Mary O'Neill, for ideas.)

Concept: Develop body awareness and spatial perception through *sensory awareness and sensory recall in character*

HOW AWARE ARE WE?

Objective: To observe closely and answer questions accurately

---

Divide the class into two groups, A and B. Each group chooses a person in their group and writes a series of twenty questions that can be answered "Yes" or "No" about the person's appearance and habits. For example:

> Are John's eyes blue?
> Does he wear glasses?
> Does he part his hair?
> If so, is it on the left side?
> Does he write left-handed?

The person Chosen by Group A leaves the room, or goes somewhere where he or she can't be seen. Group A asks Group B their set of questions. Then the person chosen by Groups B leaves, and Group B asks Group A their set of questions. The team with the most correct answers is the winner.

SHAPE UP!

Objective: To observe closely and replicate the shapes observed

Divide the class into groups of four. One person is to make a shape with his or her body. The second person adds to the shape in some way so that together they look like a single sculpture. The other two members have their backs turned until the sculpture is ready. Then they look at it very closely for about fifteen seconds. The first two return to normal positions, while the second pair make themselves into the same shape as the first pair. The first pair check to see if everything is correct. Then reverse roles.

Do the same with groups of six. Three make the statue, three duplicate it. The only rule is that no one is to climb on another person's back. Then use groups of eight, and ten, if they can handle it.

Afterward, discuss how trying to duplicate the shapes of five people is different from duplicating two people. In the larger group it is necessary for each person to be responsible for the shape created by one person, rather than knowing how everything goes together exactly.

THE CAVE

Objective: To use the senses to establish the reality of being in a cave, and to react as a character other than themselves

Materials: A record of electronic music, or some kind of dissonant music. "Poem Electronique" or "Integrales" by Edgar Varese would be appropriate.

The students each find their own place on the floor and imagine what they would do if suddenly they woke up in a cold, dark cave. Ask them to close their eyes as if they were asleep. Play music to set the "eerie" mood. While they play, sidecoach:

> *Even before you open your eyes, you begin to feel that you are in a strange place. Feel the dampness. Maybe you can hear a dripping sound. Smell the dampness. Feel the cold, hard ground under you.*
>
> *Open your eyes. It is very dark. Sit up and try to see through the darkness. Smell the mildew and the mold. Feel the walls. They are rough and uneven. Try to get a feeling of the shape and size of the cave. You run into a spider web. Everything about this place is frightening. You must find a way out of here. You must escape. Try to find a way, even though you can see no light at all.*

Let them work to the music for awhile. Some will escape, some will still be working on it when you give the signal to stop. Discuss what they saw, and felt, and heard.

Play the same thing, but this time they are to imagine they are someone different from themselves. How might a four year old react? How might an old, feeble person react? Remind them that in interesting stories, the person always encounters severe difficulties which need to be overcome.

REACTING TO A SOUND

Objective: To react to a sound, as a particular character

Materials: A recording of the sound of waves would add to the mood

Imagine you are on a beach, sleeping in the sun.
You are wakened by the sound of the waves.
How would you react?

What if you were a parent who fell asleep in the sun, while your two-year-old was playing in the waves? How would you react when you woke up?

What other characters might react to the sound of the waves in still other ways? For example, how might a non-swimmer, who was floating on a raft, respond to the waves if he or she woke up and found the raft had drifted a long way from the shore?

Discuss several possibilities for characters and what they might do.

Each person decides on a character and plays the scene according to the way they think the character would react. After they all play, simultaneously, discuss the various reactions. The point to make is that people react differently to the same stimulus, in this case the sound of waves, depending upon who they are, their past experiences, and the situation they are in.

Other sound stimuli might include a siren, strange footsteps at night, a doorbell ringing at 3:00 a.m., dishes rattling in the cupboard.

Concept: Develop body awareness and spatial perception through *pantomime*

WHERE?

Objective: To pantomime being in a specific place

Events in a play always occur in a certain place, whether it is an ordinary living room or outer space. It is up to the actors to let the audience know through their actions just where they are.

Direct the students to sit down in one large circle. The center of the circle can be any kind of place they want it to be — a jungle, a snowbank, a dungeon, anyplace. Each one should think of an idea for a place, but not say it aloud.

One person is to enter the center of the circle as if it were the particular place imagined, and do something that helps communicate where that place is, without telling. As soon as others in the circle think they know what the place is, they join the first person, doing *something else* that would be appropriate for that space. For example, if the first person establishes that he or she is snow skiing, others could enter and either ski in a different way, or build a snow man, or have a snowball fight — whatever would be appropriate to do in the snow. Before too long, almost all the students will be pantomiming in the place set by the first person.

CHARADE PANTOMIME

Objective: To pantomime activities determined by selecting cards at random

Materials: Index cards

Divide the class into four teams. Each team has four cards on which they write activities, such as building a fire, buying groceries, and so on. The cards are collected and shuffled. Each team, in turn, picks a card and quickly pantomimes the activity. The other teams try to determine what the activity is in as little time as possible. Use a stop watch to see how many seconds it takes to guess correctly.

The emphasis is on clear pantomime, so the team guessing correctly *and* the team doing the pantomime both get the number of seconds as their score. The team with the fewest number of seconds at the end, wins.

Concept: Develop body awareness and spatial perception through *emotional recall in character*

WAITING

Objective: To develop a character and express the character's feelings realistically

---

The students are to think of an adult character they find interesting — either a real person, or a type of person. The person is about to enter a bus station to catch a bus to another city for a very important reason. The students must decide on such things about the character as

the age,
occupation,
important reason for going on the bus,
personality type.

The characters walk in and take a seat to wait for the bus. They can talk to one another in character, if they wish. Tell them you will play the part of the station attendant.

After a minute or so, announce that the bus will be delayed half an hour. After a little while longer, announce that the bus has room for only five passengers. Since they all have tickes, how will they decide which five will go?

Then, later still, announce that the bus has broken down and will not be leaving at all.

Afterward, discuss how their characters felt and why.

How did different characters show their emotions?
Do people always show their emotions in real life? If not, what do they do?
What are the advantages and disadvantages of showing emotions?

SOMETHING HAPPENS

Objective: To develop a situation, based on two different emotions

Materials: Make two sets of cards, or ask the class to compose a list of words which will go on the cards.

Each card in Set 1 has a word on it that express a happy mood, such as
joyous, delighted, gay,
cheerful, glad, lucky,
jolly, exhilarated, or playful.
Words for Set 2 might include
sad, angry, anxious
quarrelsome, frustrated,
disappointed, grouchy, or glum

Divide the class into groups of three or four. Each group picks a card from each set. They are to develop a scene in which the mood changes from either the happy mood to the unhappy, or the reverse. The change of mood can come from an *outside* force, such as
a phone call, a letter,
an item in the newspaper, a person coming in,
or from one or more of the people *within* the group, such as
an announcement being made,
a quarrel, an accident.
They must decide
who they are,
where they are, and
what they are doing, as well as
what happens to change the mood.
After they have played their scenes, discuss them:
How was the change of mood made apparent?
Were the changes believable?
How could they be even more believable?

Concept: *Original dialogue*

GIBBERISH

Objective: To communicate feelings by vocal tone, pitch, volume, and rate of speed

---

If you were in a foreign country where you did not know the language, how might just the sound of a person's voice tell you that the person was sad?

Tell them that they are to describe something sad, maybe a pet dying, only they are to do it in a made-up language, called gibberish. They all speak at once.

Then ask them to tell someone who sits near them to come quickly. There is an emergency and help is needed. Again, they use gibberish.

Discuss the differences in the sound of their voices in the two situations.

In groups of six or seven, have them tell a very spooky story, using gibberish. One person starts the story, then after a couple of "sentences," the next person picks it up. The story gets more and more exciting. Finally the last person in the group ends it. Afterward, ask them how they knew when there was an exciting part of the story being told, and how they knew what the ending was like.

In the same groups, one person at a time answers the phone. They are to let their voice, actions and words convey how they feel about the person on the other end of the line. They can use English this time. Remind them to give the other (imaginery) person time to speak and really imagine what he or she is saying before responding.

The rest of the group watches and listens to see if they can tell how the person answering the phone seems to feel about the caller. The idea is to think of different attitudes and notice how they are reflected in speech.

TIMING

Objective: To vary the rate of speed, depending on what needs to be communicated

Actors need to know how the rate of speed affects the meaning of what they are saying. Have the class try out the following ideas, all together.

> *Imagine you are a mother or father explaining carefully to your three-year-old that he is not to cross the street alone. Use gibberish to talk to him.*
>
> *Now imagine that you have left him playing in the yard. You look out the window and see him step into the street. A car is coming. React in gibberish.*
>
> *What did you notice about your voice in those two situations?*
>
> *How did the rate of speed change?*
>
> *Often a person's objectives determine the rate of speed. How did the objectives of the parent differ in those two instances?*

Repeat the situations. This time they respond in English.

In pairs, let them try out this situation:

> *One person has been kidnapped and is being held for ransom. The scene begins with the kidnapper bringing the bound and gagged person in the door. The kidnapper has to go downstairs for something. The victim tries to get to the telephone to tell the operator to get the police at once.*

Give the pairs a minute to plan the setting — where the doors are, where the telephone is. Tell them not to plan an ending to the scene, but to let the ending occur spontaneously. They may use English or gibberish.

After all have played simultaneously, one or two pairs may like to show their scene to the rest of the class. Afterward, discuss the speech, with particular emphasis on rate of speed.

SWITCHING STATIONS

Objective: To practice speaking clearly and with variety in vocal inflection

Materials: Tape recorder and blank tape

Discuss commercials they have heard on the radio. In their view, what makes a good commercial?

Divide the class into groups of three or four. Each group is to plan a radio commercial which uses sound effects, as well as voices. They should practice it several times.

Then record their commercials, but interrupt them frequently, by pretending to switch stations. When you return to their "station," they should pick up right where they left off before. Listen to the tape and discuss the use of sound and voice.

ESSENTIAL ELEMENT TWO: CREATIVE DRAMA

Concept: Dramatize original stories using *pantomime*

MUSIC SETS THE MOOD

Objective: To pantomime scenes in which a particular mood is established

Materials: 1. A record which has a happy, carefree mood to it. There are many possibilities. Records by Chuck Mangione or Hap Palmer provide several options. 2. A contrasting piece of music which might suggest a mood of mystery, or struggle. Examples: *Music for Strings, Percussion and Celesta,* by Bartok: "Hall of the Mountain King," from *Peer Gynt Suite,* by Grieg; *Pictures at an Exhibition,* by Moussorgsky; *The Planets Suite,* by Holst.

Introduce: Play the first piece of music. Ask the students to close their eyes and imagine they are listening to the sound track for a movie. They are to think of what might be happening with that music as a background. Afterward, ask them to describe the mood of the music and some of the pictures they saw as they listened.

Plan: Divide the class into groups of four or five. Each group is to pantomime a scene to the music. The scenes should have a clear beginning, middle, and end. They can be very simple. For example, the recess bell rings; the students rush out on the playfield and begin to play; recess is over.

Act: All groups can play their scenes simultaneously, or they can share them, one at a time. Ask the audience to see how they capture the mood of the music.

Evaluate: Ask what the group did that fit the happy, carefree mood of the music. Did they seem to be enjoying themselves? What could be done to establish the mood even more clearly?

Plan, Act, Evaluate: Proceed in a similar way, using a contrasting piece of music, such as those suggested above. Due to the more dramatic nature of the music, it will probably suggest a more definite plot line to the students.

HALLOWEEN

Objective: To pantomime the characteristic movements of each character

Materials: Music: *Danse Macabre, Opus 40,* by Camille Saint-Saens

Introduce: Ask the students to close their eyes while they listen to the music, and decide what they think is happening at the very beginning. Play the opening portion of *Danse Macabre,* from the clock striking and into a bit of the dance.

Accept all their ideas, but the one pertinent to the music is the clock striking twelve. Play that part again. Then ask them what is special about twelve o'clock midnight on Halloween. According to legend, that is the one night of the year that ghosts, skeletons, witches, zombies, vampires and other such characters come alive and celebrate.

Tell the name of the music and explain the word "macabre." The man who composed the music was inspired by a poem call the "Dance of Death," by Henri Cazalis. (The poem is excellent for choral reading, incidently.)

Present:
> **Click, click, click . . .**
> **Death is prancing;**
> **Death, at midnight, goes a-dancing**
> **Tapping on a tomb with talon thin,**
> **Click, click, click**
> **Goes the grisly violin.**

Plan: Listen to the music.
> *What kind of beings do you see and what is the setting like?*
> *How would a skeleton move differently from a ghost?*

Try the movement just using the hands. Each student decides on what kind of creature to be and where the creature appears from, such as tombstone, or a tree. While playing the music, sidecoach:
> *Maybe you are a bit stiff at first from being still so long.*

184

How do you feel to be free for these few hours? Make your creatures show how they feel.

Suddenly the cock crows indicating it is dawn. Show what happens.

Act: *It is hard to create a skeleton or ghost with just the hands. This time use your whole body to rise from the tomb or wherever you are. Find a place and a good starting position.*

Some of the students could be playing the "grisly violins," sitting on tombstones, and watching the revelry. You may want to darken the room somewhat.

Evaluate: *What difference did you see between the way the skeletons danced and the way the ghosts danced?*

What signs did you see that they were glad to be free?

You can add to the activity by planning what the creatures might do if a couple of young children happened to come and spy on them. Use the ideas as the basis for a play.

Concept: Dramatize original stories using *improvisation* which focuses on the *setting* and *time of plot*

PLOT: SETTING

Objective: To create a scene, using a specific setting

Materials: Cards with places, or settings, written on them, such as a dark forest, a supermarket, an airplane in flight, a deserted house, a lake, a telephone booth.

Warm-up: Use the **Where?** activity on page 175.

Introduce: It is important to establish where a scene or play takes place. In fact, the setting often affects what happens in the plot.

Divide the class into groups of three or four. Each group is to invent a plot with a problem, complications and solutions, around the sentence "Help me." Each group will be given a card with the name of a place written on it. The action of the scene will occur in that particular place.

Plan: They are to work out what happens in the scene and then plan the details of the place they are in. They can rearrange chairs, tables and other things in the room, if that will help show where they are. Sometimes a chair or table can be used in a way that shows it is something else. For example, some chairs put together could be a log crossing a ravine, or a sofa. After they have planned the action and the setting, they should rehearse the scene once or twice.

Act: One group shows its scene while the rest watch. The audience is to try to get a feeling for what the setting is and watch for as many specific details about the place as they can.

Evaluate: After each scene, instead of discussing what happened and what

186

the setting was, give each person a piece of paper. Tell them to make a quick sketch of the place they envisioned because of what they saw the players do. Allow only two minutes for the sketch. Artistry is not important. They can use symbols and label them if they wish. The people who played the scene should make a sketch, too. If their ideas are quite different, they might discuss why it is necessary to work with the same basic plan.

PLOT: TIME

Objective: To create a scene in which the action occurs at a certain time

Materials: Cards with a certain time written on them: 15,000 B.C.; 3000 A.D.; New Year's Eve; Halloween; 3:00 a.m.; 4:00 p.m.

Introduce: Briefly discuss things that are different today from when their grandparents were children. *When* something occurs can be very important to the plot of a play. Even the hour of the day can make a big difference. For example, if you hear a knock on the door at three o'clock in the afternoon, you would think nothing of it. If you hear a knock at three in the morning, that would be quite a different matter.

Plan: Divide the class into groups of three or four. Each group is to improvise a scene around the same object, such as a glistening stone. You may or may not have the object on hand. Each group is given a card with a certain time in which the action of the scene is to occur. Allow them time to work on the scene, deciding
> *who* the characters are,
> *where* they are,
> *what* happens.

Act: Each group acts its scene before the rest of the class, without telling them what the time of their scene is. Ask the audience to watch for the ways the time of the scene affects the action.

Evaluate: Use the question directed to the audience before the scenes were played.

WHO, WHERE, WHEN

Objective: To improvise scenes, using given characters, settings, and times

Materials: Blank index cards — three for each student

Warm-up and Introduce: Tell the students to start walking briskly around the room, with no talking. While they walk, call out various characters. When a character is named, they are to do something immediately that they think that character would do. After they do the character action for a few seconds, they resume walking until the next character is called. A drum beat for the walking would be effective. Examples:

> an old man,
> a firefighter,
> a doctor,
> a teacher,
> a dog,
> a frog,
> a sprinkler,
> a surfboard.

There are so many interesting characters and places and situations to make plays about. Pass out three cards to each person. They should label each card first:

> Who, on one card;
> Where, on another;
> When, on the last.

Then they are to think of an interesting character or group of characters and write the idea on the "who" card. For example, astronauts. Collect the "who" cards. Do the same with the "when" and "where" cards, keeping each of the three piles separate.

Plan: Divide the class into groups of four or five. Each group picks a card at random from each pile. Then the groups develop scenes, using the information from the cards. All they need to decide is what the characters are doing. Allow a brief planning period.

Act: Each group shows its scene for the class, without having played it through beforehand. Encourage them to stay in character during the scene even if something unexpected comes up. They need to react to each other as their characters would.

Evaluate: Ask the audience if they could identify who, where, when for each scene. Was the action of the scene (the "what") clear? How might the scene be improved?

The cards can be used many times, both for drama and for creative writing.

Concept: Dramatize original stories focusing on *characterization,* and especially *speech* which reveals character

---

BEYOND WORDS

Objective: To communicate through vocal pitch, intensity, volume, and rate of speed, as well as words

---

Introduce: Discuss how a person's voice lets one know what kind of mood he or she is in. Ask the students how they can tell what kind of mood someone in their family is in at certain times.

Tell the students to close their eyes and listen to some sounds you are going to make. They are to see whether they can tell what kind of mood you are trying to communicate. Use a series of repetitive syllables, such as bum-bum-bum, or use the letters of the alphabet. Say them in a lilting, joyful manner, as if you are very happy. Afterward, ask what it was about your voice that let them know what mood you were expressing. For example,

Was there variation in pitch?
Was it loud or soft?
Was it fast or slow?

Then have them try expressing happiness all together, using gibberish.

Next, ask them to remember a time when they were really scared. They are to use the same sounds, no words, but make it seem as if they are scared.

Do the same thing with anger. Then discuss the differences in the way the voice was used in the different situations.

Plan and Act: Tell them to imagine that it is their birthday. They are opening a present and it turns out to be something they wanted very much. When you give the signal, they open the present, and run to someone else to tell them about the gift. They can use words, but they are to use their voices to communicate how they feel about their present.

Evaluate: How did the voices show their excitement?

Plan and Act: Now, ask them to imagine it is their birthday once again. They are counting on getting one special item they asked for. They have the present; it is the right size and weight for what they expect. They open the package, but it is not what they wanted at all. They are to let their voices show how they would feel if no one were around to watch and hear them.

Evaluate: Discuss the quality of the sounds.

DIFFERENT INTENTIONS

Objective: To say the same words in a variety of ways to communicate different feelings

---

Introduce: Ask the students to name as many different feelings as they can. List them on the board. A beginning list might include

> excitement,
> anger,
> anxiety,
> boredom,
> sadness.

Then write a simple sentence on the board, such as "I want that pen," or "Go home."

Act: The students are to say the sentence in a variety of ways to show various feelings. They should choose a feeling from the list, but not tell the class what it is.

Evaluate: What feeling did the person convey?

Concept: Dramatize original stories using *situation role playing*

REACTIONS

Objective: To improvise a scene in which characters react
differently to the same situation

Introduce: Questions for the class:

*If someone comes up to you and remarks about how great your new
shirt or blouse looks, how do you react?*

How do you feel inside?

*If someone at home said, "Can't you ever do anything right?" how
would you react?*

How would you feel toward the person?

Sometimes people have different reactions to the same thing. One person
may scream and run from a spider. A second person may want to examine it
more closely to see what kind it is. A third person may catch it to scare
someone. A fourth person may step on it.

[handwritten right margin: Spider 1. Run 2. Examine 3. Catch 4. Kill *]*

Plan: This lesson involves working on a scene in which there are different
reactions. Divide the class into groups of three or four. Describe the situation:

*One person has just had a haircut. It is very short. This is the first
morning at school after the haircut and the person is feeling very
self-conscious.*

*Two or three classmates come over. Each has a different reaction to
the way the hair looks.*

Each group is to plan a scene with conflict and decide how it will end.

Act: All groups can act simultaneously, or each group can act in front of the
rest of the class. If the latter, tell the audience to watch for the different
reactions and notice how the reaction of the student with the haircut in turn
affects the way the classmates respond.

CROWDS

Objective: To enact a crowd scene and become aware of how people stimulate one another in a crowd

---

Introduce: Choose a situation, or have the class choose a situation, which the students are currently very much aware of and which they care about. Or choose a situation which they could easily imagine and would react to strongly. Examples:

A school rule which they feel is very unfair;

School continuing until 5 p.m., or year around attendance;

A ban on extracurricular activities;

The closing of all beaches;

Teachers going through student lockers each day.

Plan: One rule in the playing: *no physical contact.* Decide on the setting for the situation — the school hallway, outside, or some other appropriate place. Before they begin playing, remind them to stay in character at all times. It is important for each one to make it seem as if he or she cares deeply about the situation at all times.

Play: You tell them verbally when to take each of the following steps.

1. In pairs, they are to begin discussing the issue, grumbling about it. They can walk as they talk.
2. Then each pair joins another pair and they continue the discussion. You can use a cymbal or a drum to indicate when they should merge with other groups.
3. Then fours join other fours, eights join eights. The discussion

becomes more heated. This continues until the entire class is together in one group and they decide they must take some action.

If they decide to go to the governor or principal, you can take the role of that person. You can help heighten their antagonism by sending word that you will not see them at first. When you do see them, keep a desk or table between you and the crowd. The resolution depends upon the circumstances being played out. There may be a stalemate.

Evaluate: Discuss their feelings at the beginning of the scene as opposed to the end. There may be new awareness of crowd psychology which they will be eager to discuss, relating to current demonstrations they may have read about and seen on television.

MOVE ONE CHAIR

Objective: To enact situations from various viewpoints in order to better understand other people's view and feelings

This is a game in which students have the opportunity to play several different characters. Set up as many chairs as there are characters in a given scene. Each student sits in a chair and begins playing a certain role. When you say "Change," the students move to the chair on their left, and begin playing the role that was played by the person sitting in that particular chair before. They should pick up where the other person was, even if it was in mid-sentence. You can say "change" any number of times, giving more than one chance to play a given role in a scene. After they have played for awhile, tell them to find a way to end the scene.

The following is a beginning list of situations which may be meaningful to your class. You and the class may come up with other situations which are relevant to them. They must be acted with sincerity and concentration, if the objective is to be accomplished.

1. A new student enters school in the middle of the year. He or she is shy and other students don't include the new student in their activities.

2. A student who was well liked at school suddenly seems to have a change of personality and makes hurtful remarks to his or her friends, and doesn't do homework assignments. After some time, it is discovered that there are problems at home.

3. A student has asked for a certain present from the family. It is something the student has counted on for a long time. It is quite expensive. The family has come into financial difficulties and can't buy the present. They call their child in to talk about it.

4. A child finds $10 dollars on the counter at home. It is with a grocery list. The child is seen by a brother as she or he takes the money. The brother theatens to tell the parents if the money is not returned.

5. A student is caught cheating on a test. The principal has called a meeting

of the student, the student's parent, and the teacher. The parent thinks the student can do no wrong.

6. There are three children and one parent. The oldest child stayed out too late. The parent decides to punish the child. One of the children is on the side of the parent; the other is on the side of the oldest child.

7. A mother is talking to her three children. She wants to go away on vacation, leaving the children alone.

ESSENTIAL ELEMENT THREE:
AESTHETIC GROWTH THROUGH THE APPRECIATION
OF THEATRICAL EVENTS

Concept: View theatrical events, emphasizing
*analysis of how speech reveals character;
recognition of the kind of conflict;
suggestions for alternative courses of action;
evaluation and aesthetic judgements*

NOTE: Viewing theatrical events means going to a theatre, or seeing a performance by a touring group who comes to the school. Most theatre companies will provide study guides to help prepare the students for a performance, and to further their understanding through follow-up activities.

The following lesson is based on a play, *The Hammer of Thor,* included here. The lesson serves as a model of how to analyze certain aspects of a play. The play can be either performed by the students, or simply read out loud.

THE HAMMER OF THOR

Objectives:
1. To analyze how speech and the use of the voice can reveal character
2. To recognize the kind of conflict represented in the plot
3. To make suggestions for alternative courses of action
4. To evaluate and make aesthetic judgments

Introduce: Ask the students to give examples of times when they may have lost something of great value to them, and to describe how they felt about it.

Suppose you discovered that someone you know took the item. What would you do?

The play they are about to read deals with that situation. It is an old Norse myth. The gods in Norse mythology were very powerful, but they had many human characteristics as well. They also had enemies who wanted to conquer them and take away their power.

Tell the students to be aware of the physical characteristics of the characters as they read the play, particularly the way their voices might sound.

Present: *THE HAMMER OF THOR*

CHARACTERS

Thor, the strongest god, protector of Asgard where the gods live
Sif, Thor's wife
Freya, a beautiful goddess
Heimdall, guard of Asgard
Loki, a god who gets into mischief
Thrym, a wicked giant
Thrym's Servants (about ten)
Narrator

This play has two scenes.
Scene 1: Asgard, the home of the gods
Scene 2: Thrym's banquet hall

SCENE 1

NARRATOR:
One of the most colorful gods of Norse legends was Thor. Thor was a huge god with flashing red eyes and a long red beard. His most valued possession was his mighty hammer, which was extremely powerful and so heavy that it took ten men to lift it. No matter who Thor threw the hammer at, it never missed its mark. And after it hit, it returned to Thor's hand. Because of the hammer's accuracy and power, Thor was able to protect Asgard, where the gods lived, from all its terrible enemies. But, one morning, disaster hit Asgard as Thor awoke to find his hammer missing.

THOR: (Sound effect of things being crashed and thrown around)
My hammer! My hammer! Where is my hammer?

SIF:

Calm down, calm down. Now it must be somewhere. Where did you put it?

THOR:

If I knew where I put it, I wouldn't be looking for it now!

SIF:

I know, but where did you put it last?

THOR: (Disgusted)

Don't ask such foolish questions. Look for it! I must have dropped it somewhere.

SIF:

All right, all right!

NARRATOR:

Because of the shouting and crashing around Thor was doing, the other gods and goddesses were worried and came running to find out what had happened.

FREYA:

What's wrong, Thor? What's happening? Are you all right?

THOR:

Of course I'm all right! But I've lost my hammer!

HEIMDALL:

How terrible! Without it, how shall we keep the giants away?

LOKI:

We can't. The giant Thrym, our enemy, already has it.

THOR:

Loki! How do you know this? Where have you been? Have you seen my hammer?

HEIMDALL:

Quiet, Thor! Let Loki talk.

LOKI:

If you will all be quiet, I'll tell you. I was flying over Giantland and I saw Thrym on a hill. He called to me as I flew over. "Good morning, Loki. How is everything in Asgard?" "Fine," I answered. "Then no one realizes that Thor's hammer is gone yet," Thrym said. "What do you mean?" I asked. And he told me that he had taken Thor's hammer and hidden it eight miles deep in the earth — and that's not all. He will never give it back unless Freya becomes his bride.

(Pause — everyone looks at Freya.)

THOR:

Don't just stand there, Freya, get into your wedding clothes and hurry up. I've got to get my hammer back at once!

FREYA: (Very angry)

Never! I will never become Thrym's bride. I don't care what the reason is. He is big and fat and stupid and ugly and I will not marry him!

THOR:

This is no time to be choosy. We must get the hammer or we may lose Asgard to the giants!

FREYA: (Crying)

I won't go. I just can't do it.

HEIMDALL:

I have an idea. If Freya will not go, why not dress Thor up as a bride and send him as Freya? After all, Thrym is so ugly himself, Thor would seem beautiful to him.

LOKI:

Marvellous, marvellous! We can put a veil over his beard and give him Freya's beautiful necklace to wear. Find a dress for him, too, Sif. (Sif goes to a closet and gets some clothes. As soon as she gets them she and Freya begin to dress Thor. Thor does not cooperate very well.)

THOR:

Stop it! I will not make such a fool out of myself. I refuse to do this.

FREYA: (Mocking Thor)
This is no time to be so choosy.

HEIMDALL:
Now, Thor, you must do it! And Loki can go as your maid and talk to Thrym so he can't hear your booming voice. You just be sure to keep your face covered with your veil as if you are very shy.

THOR: (Shouting)
No! I won't do it! Loki has caused us enough trouble in the past and I won't let him speak for me now! Besides, if I wear this dress, all of Asgard will laugh at me.

LOKI:
Thor, we have no choice. Freya won't go, and if you really want your hammer back you must go yourself and get it!

THOR:
Oh, all right. If I must, I must. But you stop laughing, Freya, if you know what's good for you.

FREYA: (Laughing)
But just wait until you see how funny you look! Don't breathe too hard or you'll pop the seams on your beautiful white dress! It's too bad brides don't wear red dresses. Then your dress would match your lovely red eyes.

(Everyone laughs except Thor who frowns and shakes his fist at the others.)

SCENE 2

NARRATOR:
So Loki and Thor set out for Thrym's home dressed as Freya and her maid. Thrym had made everything ready for his bride. The floors were swept clean, a wonderful feast had been prepared, and Thrym himself was dressed in his best robe. As Loki and Thor drove up in their carriage, Thrym rushed forward to meet them.

204

THRYM:

Welcome, lovely Freya! I've waited so long and impatiently for your arrival. Let me help you. (Thrym takes Thor's hand. Thor grabs his hand away as quickly as he can.)
My goodness, Freya, you have such large hands and you have such broad shoulders too. You are larger than I thought you would be.

LOKI:

That is a sign of true beauty, sir. Look how wide and handsome *you* are!

THRYM:

Oh, my, do you really think so? Say, why doesn't your mistress speak?

LOKI:

Oh, she is much too shy. I will speak for her.

THRYM:

Well, come into the feasting hall and sit right here next to me, lovely Freya. Now, eat whatever you like, fair one. If you are still too shy to speak, just point at the things you would like to eat. Here comes a platter of fish.
(Servants bring in great trays of food.)
Here is the roast beef. Here is a tray of strawberries as large as watermelons. Ah, here comes a mountain of mashed potatoes. And a pitcher of ale to quench your thirst.

NARRATOR: (Thrym, Loki, and Thor pantomime eating while Narrator speaks)
Thor eats and eats and eats — eight salmon, one whole ox, ten bushels of mashed potatoes, and forty gallons of ale. Loki keeps nudging Thor to try to stop him from eating so much but nothing can stop Thor's appetite. The huge appetite startles Thrym.

LOKI: (Whispering to Thor)
Slow down! Don't eat so much. Remember, you are Freya!

THRYM:
Never in my life have I seen anyone eat so much!

LOKI:

Well, you would be starving too if you hadn't eaten for eight days. Freya has been so excited since she got your message that she hasn't been able to eat a thing!

THRYM:

She was really so excited? I must give her a kiss. Let me lift her veil and see her lovely face!
(Thor glares at Thrym. Thrym gasps.)
Oh, her eyes — I only saw her eyes but they are so *red* and piercing!

LOKI:

Well, she also hasn't slept for eight nights because she was thinking about you! No wonder her blue eyes have turned red.
(Thor continues to eat, paying no attention to Thrym and Loki. Loki continues to nudge Thor to try to make him stop eating.)

THRYM:

Are her eyes really blue?

LOKI:

Oh my, yes. As blue as the skies on a lovely summer day.

THRYM:

Then let us be married right now. You, servants, clear the table for the wedding ceremony.

LOKI:

Wait, Thrym. Freya will not go through with the ceremony until you bring Thor's hammer here and she can touch it with her own hand.

THRYM:

We can do that later. (Thor leans toward Loki and whispers in Loki's ear.)

LOKI:

No. Freya refuses to be married until after she sees the hammer. I think you'd better humor her, Thrym. She can be very stubborn.

THRYM:

All right, all right. You servants, go fetch the hammer for Freya.
(It takes all the servants to carry the hammer. When it is brought, Thor grabs it.)

206

THOR: (Standing up and tearing off the bridal veil.)
Now I have the hammer, Thrym. This is the end for you and your kind.

THRYM: (Shocked)
Thor! You are not Freya! You are Thor!

THOR:
Yes, I am Thor! And this is for you, Thrym!

NARRATOR (Action is pantomimed as Narrator speaks)
As he said those words, Thor hurled his hammer at the wall of the banquet room. The timbers of the banquet hall creaked and groaned as they toppled over on the giants. Thor and Loki walked out of the ruins, smiling while they listened to the yells and shrieks of the terrified giants.

Discuss the characters: These questions can help the students plan to perform the play, or they can be used to analyze the reading.

Thor:
What did the play say about what Thor looks like and sounds like?

How would his voice help the audience know he was one of the most powerful of the gods?

Why is the hammer so important to Thor?

Why doesn't Thor want to dress up like a bride?

Why doesn't he talk at the wedding feast?

Why does he eat so much?

Sif:
How does she feel toward Thor?

How does she try to help him find the hammer?

How could her voice reveal how she feels?

How do you think she feels when she helps Thor dress as a bride?

Freya:
Why does the thought of marrying Thrym make Freya so angry?

How would her voice reflect how she feels?

Why does she laugh when Thor gets dressed up?

Heimdall:

    He is the guard of Asgard. What do you think he looks like?

    How do you know he is as clever as he is strong?

    What do you think his voice sounds like?

Loki:

    When Loki tells about talking with Thrym, he imitates Thrym's voice. How might that sound?

    Do you think Loki minds dressing like the bridesmaid?

    How does he make his voice sound like a girl's when he talks to Thrym?

    What does he do to try to be charming to Thrym? How would his voice sound?

    How do you know he gets nervous when Thrym notices how much Thor has eaten and how red his eyes are?

Thrym:

    What do you think Thrym looks like?

    Why did he steal the hammer?

    Why does he want to marry Freya? What does he do that shows how anxious he is to marry her?

    What does his voice sound like when he thinks he is talking to his bride?

    How does he react to Loki's flattery?

    What does he think when he sees that the bride is Thor not Freya? How would his voice reveal his feelings?

Servants:

    Why are the servants very important in this play?

    How do they bring in the heaping platters of food?

    How do they bring in the hammer, to show how heavy it is?

What sounds might they make when the walls fall in at the end?

Discuss the conflict and alternative courses of action:

What kind of conflict is represented in this play? Is it person versus person, person versus the environment, or person against him or herself?

    What is Thor's objective — what does he want?

    What is Thrym's objective? Why does this cause the conflict?

Do you think Thrym really planned to give the hammer back to Thor? (Remember that the giants were always trying to overtake the gods.)

What other courses of action might Thor have taken instead of dressing up like Freya? How would other courses of action change the play? Would it be as interesting, or more interesting? Would it have been as funny?

Staging Considerations: You can discuss these, whether or not the class performs the play. Tell them to keep the audience in mind as they think of the following problems:

> *Will you use off-stage sound effects for the beginning of the play, or do you want Thor to make all the noise himself?*
>
> *What parts of the stage can Thor and Sif use when they are looking frantically for the hammer?*
>
> *The hammer is so large that it is probably better to pantomime using it. How can the servants make it seem very heavy?*
>
> *What could be used for Thor's dress, veil and Freya's necklace?*
>
> *What can be used for the banquet table? Who brings it in?*
>
> *Where will the servants stand after they serve the food?*
>
> *Do you want to use sound effects for the end, when the banquet hall falls down? How can pantomime help communicate what happens when the walls fall down?*

Evaluating and making aesthetic judgments: Since a theatrical event is a thing witnessed, not just read, one must see a performance in order to judge it. If the class has actually performed *The Hammer of Thor*, you can evaluate it. If not, talk about a television show or movie most of them have seen. Questions such as the following can be tailored to most shows:

> *1. What did you like about it?*
>
> *2. Were the characters believable within the context of the plot? Were their objectives clear? Did you know how they felt about what was happening at any given time? How did the sound of their voices help communicate what their characters were like?*
>
> *3. Did the conflict and tension build through the play until the climax was reached?*

4. *How did the costumes help you know what the characters were like?*

5. *How did the scenery help you know where the action was taking place?*

6. *What might be done differently to improve the play?*

SEEING A PLAY

Objective: To evaluate and make aesthetic judgments about a
live theatre production.

Before the play: Most theatre companies provide a study guide for
teachers to use with students both before and after the play. Such a guide can
help prepare the students for seeing the play. The better prepared they are,
the more likely they are to enjoy the performance. They will anticipate what is
about to happen, and know something about the plot and characters.

If the play is based on a story or book, you may want to read the story, or
excerpts from the story, to the class. They will understand the play better, if
they know the basic plot beforehand.

You might want the students to act out a few of the more exciting scenes
before they see the play. You could also ask them to recall and enact times
when they were afraid, or sad, or joyous, just like the characters in the story.
They will find it interesting to compare what they did with what the actors do
in the play.

If there are any concepts or words you think they might not understand,
these should be reviewed beforehand.

If the play is set during a particular historical period, you might want to
bring in some pictures of the period. Discuss the types of clothes people
wore, what kind of transportation they used, what kind of homes they lived in.

After the Play: Providing a variety of ways for students to respond to
seeing the play is important to reinforce their learning. If you were given a
study guide, you may find follow-up suggestions that will appeal to your class.
The following is a list of activities which many teachers have found useful.
Obviously these are "generic" suggestions, and you would want to tailor them
to fit the particular play the class saw.

1. Draw your favorite character, or the most exciting scene.
2. Draw the set.

3. Dramatize:
   a. Show how each of the characters walked.
   b. Choose one scene from the play to act out. Why was that scene selected?
   c. Act out a different ending for the play.
   d. Act out a scene from another story which shows courage, feeling afraid, reaching a goal — whatever is appropriate to the play that was seen.
4. Discuss:
   a. What was the most exciting part of the play? How did you feel during that part?
   b. Who was your favorite character? What did you like about him or her?
   c. What was the objective of each character?
   d. Did you know how they felt about what was happening at any given time?
   e. How did the sound of their voices help communicate what the characters were like?
   f. Select three words to describe each of the characters in the play.
   g. How was the play the same, or different, from the story or book it was based on? (If appropriate.)
   h. What was the main conflict? Did the conflict and tension build through the play until the climax was reached? How was the conflict resolved?
   i. What could have happened to change the ending?
   j. How did the designers of the scenery, costumes, props and lights use their imaginations?
   k. How did the costumes help you know what the characters were like?
   l. How did the scenery help you know where the action was taking place?
   m. If you were the director, what might you have done differently to improve the play?

Concept: Recognize similarities and differences among television, film and theatre, emphasizing *camera angles* and *audience position*

LIGHTS, CAMERA, ACTION!

Objective: To recognize similarities and differences among television, film and live theatre, with regard to the effect of camera angles and the position of the audience.

Materials: If at all possible, use a video tape recorder, or a movie camera. Also use viewfinders which can be made from stiff paper, with a half inch square cut in the middle.

Introduce: Use the *The Hammer of Thor* as the basis for discussion. Ask the children to imagine they were seeing *The Hammer of Thor* on television.

How might it be different from seeing the play in a theatre?

One difference is that the camera can focus on one person at a time to watch what the person is doing, or to see how he or she is reacting to something that happened. The camera can zoom in for a close up of just one part of a person, such as the person's face. The camera actually tells us what to watch — it becomes our eyes.

In the theatre, we usually see several characters at once, and we have to choose what or who we are going to watch at any given time. Usually we watch the person who is talking or moving on the stage.

How does the position of the audience make a difference about what is done?

Think of sitting in a theatre. How close are the actors to you?

There is usually quite a lot of distance between the actors and the audience.

*Now think of sitting in a movie house. The **screen** may be some*

213

distance away, but how close do the actors seem?

In the theatre, actors often need to use bigger movements, gestures and voices so that the audience will see and hear what is going on.

In the movies the actors can use very natural movements and the camera will see that for us. In fact, in the movies, the characters are really much bigger on screen than in real life. If the actors exaggerated their movements or spoke very loudly they would seem grotesque.

Also, in the theatre, the audience is seated facing the stage. The actors need to make sure that the audience sees their faces most of the time. They rarely talk with their backs to the audience. In film, the camera can move around and the microphone can pick up voices no matter where the actors are.

Plan and Act: Use Scene 2, from *The Hammer of Thor,* where Thor, Thrym and Loki are seated at the banquet table. Ask three students to act out the scene. As the class watches, ask them to think of camera angles and close-ups that would help the scene if it were to be on television. For example, how would they film the following?

Thor's eating
Loki's nudging him
Thor's flashing eyes when Thrym wants to kiss him

Replay the scene, with several students using viewfinders, imagining they are using a camera to film the scene. They can position themselves far away, move in close or move around the actors while they are playing the scene.

If you have a video camera, give several children the opportunity to film the scene. They can stop the scene at any time, and shoot portions again from different angles. If there is an editing device, they can even do that later. But, if not, they will still see the effect of different camera angles.

Evaluate: Play the video tape and ask them what worked well and what changes they might suggest. If you are working without a camera, talk about the kind of camera shots they imagined. Then ask them to review the differences and similarities in a play that might be done on television, film and in the theatre.

214

215

216

Chapter V:
OTHER SUBJECTS OTHER POPULATIONS

This chapter is divided into two parts. Part One provides suggestions for using drama to teach essential elements in English language arts, mathematics, science, health, physical education, fine arts, social studies, and other languages. Part Two discusses drama with other populations, more specifically, students with special needs — the academically gifted, the learning disabled, the physically disabled, the emotionally troubled, the culturally different, and the economically deprived.

Part One
CORRELATING DRAMA WITH OTHER SUBJECT AREAS

Drama can be used as an effective teaching tool for other subject areas, as well as being an important subject in its own right. However, it is important that the students have experiences in drama as a subject, first, before applying the tool to other curriculum areas. Just as a child must learn to recognize and use numbers before applying them to solve problems, so the child must learn some of the essential elements of theatre arts before applying them to other subjects.

Drama is an effective teaching tool because it causes the student to become physically, mentally and emotionally involved in the subject being studied. Because of this involvement, students generally remember more about the subject. Some students who have difficulty grasping a concept through traditional teaching methods, will understand the concept when it is taught through drama. An additional bonus is that students find learning through drama *fun!*

ENGLISH LANGUAGE ARTS

Many of the essential elements of English language arts are already so closely allied with the theatre arts lessons included in this book that, by using the drama lessons, you will be teaching essential elements in both theatre arts and language arts. These will be noted under the appropriate essential element for language arts.

The following suggestions can be used and modified according to the grade level being taught. You may also find that a particular activity can be adapted to teach a different essential element from the one stated here.

Essential Element: Listening

Concept: <u>Listen to appreciate sound for each letter of the alphabet and devices of rhythm, rhyme, alliteration, and onomatopoeia</u>

1. Each student, in turn, says "I'm going exploring today." Then the student says his or her name and pantomimes an object to take along which begins with the first sound of the name. For example, "My name is Carlos, and I'm taking a (pantomime a camera)." The rest of the class guesses what Carlos has pantomimed.

2. Each student says his or her name, and then does a series of movements which are the same in number as the syllables in the name. For example, Maria might (1) put her arms straight up, (2) clap, (3) stretch her left arm out. The class repeats her movement.

3. The name is said, followed by a rhyming word, or nonsense syllables. For example, Andre — hombre.

4. Divide the class into pairs or threes. Each group is to decide on an animal. After they have decided, tell them they are to write a sentence about that animal, using as many alliterations as possible. Then they act it out and the class tries to determine both the animal and the alliterations. For example, "The tired turtle trudged to town."

Concept: <u>Employ active listening in a variety of situations</u>

All the lessons in this book require active listening either to the teacher or to other students. In many instances the students are listening to know how and when their characters must respond during an improvisation.

218

Concept: <u>Select the information needed from an oral presentation</u>

Many of the lessons in this book require students to listen to literary presentations or improvised scenes, in order to answer specific questions afterward.

Concept: <u>Detect the use of propaganda and overgeneralization</u>

Ask the students to watch commercials to find examples of propaganda and overgeneralization. Then, in groups have them create a commercial, using propaganda and overgeneralization. After they show their commercials to the class, ask the class to state what was propaganda and overgeneralization.

If you have a video cassette camera, you may want to tape the commercials.

Concept: <u>Determine a speaker's motive, bias, and point of view</u>

The word "motive" is similar to the word "objective" used in this book. It refers to what a given character wants to do. Whenever students are creating a character, they must decide on the objective of the character. The concept of character objectives is introduced in Chapter Two in this book.

In Chapter Four, the section on "situation role playing" lends itself to analyzing bias and point of view.

Essential Element: Speaking

Concept: <u>Develop fluency in using oral language to communicate effectively</u>

You will find that the lessons in this book deal with two or more communication skills, in which children are provided opportunities to

engage in creative drama activities and nonverbal communication;

use a variety of words to express feelings and ideas;

make organized oral presentations;

participate in group problem-solving activities;

manipulate articulation, rate, volume, and physical movement in oral presentations; and

respond to thoughts expressed by others through clarifying, qualifying, and extending ideas.

Concept: <u>Speak to persuade, using a brief set of reasons</u>

219

The students work in pairs in situations such as the following:

> One student wants to see a movie, the other wants to play softball.
>
> They have found a $10 bill. One wants to turn it in; the other wants to keep it, giving $5 to the friend.
>
> One is a student, the other a teacher. The student is trying to persuade the teacher that a grade should be higher than it is.
>
> A child is trying to persuade a parent to let him or her give a party.
>
> One student is trying to get another to share lunch.

Concept: <u>Speak to entertain</u>

The lessons in this book provide many opportunities to present stories and plays for entertainment.

Essential Element: Reading

Concept: <u>Use comprehension skills to gain meaning from what is read: arrange events in sequential order, understand cause and effect relationships, predict probable future outcomes or actions, evaluate and make judgments</u>

Duplicate part of a short story for the students. In groups, ask them to discuss what they think will happen next, and act it out for the rest of the class.

In the creative drama lessons for Grades Five and Six, students are continually planning scenes in which they are focusing on plot development and the logical progression of what happens. Although they are not *reading* to do this, they are gaining experiences in prediction which can apply to their reading, with assistance from the teacher.

The plot development lessons also relate directly to the concept of understanding cause and effect relationships, as well as to arranging events in sequential order including time and degree of importance.

The section on "Evaluation and Aesthetic judgements," in Grades Five and Six, is a corollary of the concept in which students are to evaluate and make judgements about their reading.

Concept: <u>Develop literary appreciation skills to provide personal enjoyment; recognize that simile and metaphor involve comparison</u>

Part 1. Ask the students to move like a stalking cat. Then ask them to recall fog, and describe how it moves. Ask them to try to move like fog. The music, "Neptune," from *The Planets Suite,* by Holst, provides an excellent background for fog movement. Ask them to compare the movements of a cat and the movement of fog. How are they alike?

Read the poem, "Fog," by Carl Sandburg.

> **The fog comes**
> **on little cat feet.**
>
> **It sits looking**
> **over harbor and city**
> **on silent haunches**
> **and then moves on.**

Ask them questions to prepare them for acting the poem:

> *What words did Sandburg use that compared fog to a cat?*
> *What do you suppose the fog is watching? Might it see anything unusual?*
> *Where would it like to go so that it might see better?*
> *How does it move?*
> *What happens to fog when the sun comes out?*

Play the music again. The students are to be fog with catlike movements, moving in on the city and watching what is happening. After they have played for a couple of minutes, tell them the sun is beginning to break through, and the fog gradually evaporates into the air.

Discuss the difference between metaphor and simile and ask them which one was used by Sandburg.

Part 2. Ask the students to name other weather conditions and list them on the board. Divide the class into groups of three. Each group is to choose one of the weather conditions and think of an appropriate animal metaphor for it. They list words that compare the two. In fact, they can even write a poem — either using the Sandburg poem as a model, or coming up with one of their own.

Each group acts out their metaphor for the rest of the class. If they have written a poem, ask them to say the poem first, and then act it out.

Ask the class what two things were being compared, and whether the poem used metaphor or simile. If the poem used metaphor, ask them how they could change it so it was a simile, and the reverse for those that used a simile.

Concept: <u>Develop literary appreciation skills, recognizing personification as a literary device</u>

Use animal cartoons as a basis for discussing personification. In small groups, ask them to plan and act out a short scene, using animals who behave like humans do, but still keeping their basic animal shapes and movements.

Concept: <u>Develop literary appreciation skills, recognition differences in first and third person point of view</u>

In groups, ask the students to plan an interview situation involved around the "Scene of the Crime." One person plays the victim, one or two others play the witnesses and one is the interviewer.

When watching the scenes, direct the students to notice the way the event is described, and the pronouns used by each person.

Concept: <u>Develop literary appreciation skills, describing the time and setting of the story</u>

Time and setting are important to any story, scene, or improvisation. Many of the lessons in this book ask where and when the action takes place. In Chapter Four, there are specific lessons dealing with setting and time.

Concept: <u>Explain and relate the feelings and emotions of characters</u>

This concept is applied in all the creative drama lessons.

Essential Element: Writing

Many of the drama lessons in this book lend themselves to having the students write following their acting. Written expression often becomes more imaginative, vivid and colorful, following dramatization. In fact, the students are sometimes able to describe the dramatization in much more detail than was actually observed in their acting. The biggest danger comes from over-using this technique. If the students begin to realize that every time they do drama, they are going to have to write, they will lose their enthusiasm for both drama and writing.

Essential Element: Language

Concept: <u>Develop skills in using modifiers correctly</u>

1. Play the modifier game. Students walk around the room. You call on one student to suggest an adverb. Students modify their walking accordingly. Examples might include proudly, anxiously, angrily, belligerently. Encourage them to think of interesting adverbs. This can help expand vocabularies.

A similar activity can be done with adjectives. For example, the timid boy, the cocky girl, the ferocious lion.

2. With the assistance of the class, ask them to make a set of action (verb) cards and a set of adverb cards. In pairs or threes, each group picks a verb card and an adverb card at random. They are to pantomime the appropriate action and the class tries to determine what the words were.

This activity can be adapted to using nouns and adjectives.

MATHEMATICS

Essential Element: The basic operations on numbers

The "Machine Game" can be used effectly as a skill drill for all basic operations. Basically, the students create a human "Math Machine," using their bodies for the parts. The machine can be very simple, or quite complicated. The essential parts include a place for input, where the problem is put in (usually verbally), and a place for output. Some students like to form a calculator, with students responsible for each number, each of the signs, and an answer display. Other students have created a machine in which the imagined internal workings are displayed through movement and sound, until the answer is arrived at. Once a workable machine has been created, it can be used over and over again. Students vary which parts of the machine they play.

Essential Element: The use of probability and statistics to collect and interpret data

Concept: <u>Collect data and use to construct graphs</u>

The "Sleuth Game" can be used to add interest to collecting data, and constructing graphs. Divide the class into "sleuth teams" of two or three students. Each team is given a problem, which is to be kept secret. Therefore, they need to do their investigating in a way that the other students don't know what it is they are looking for. After the investigations, they construct a graph which they may explain to the class, or which the other members of the class may interpret.

The following are just a few examples. No doubt, you will be able to think of many more.

> *How many students are likely to wear white socks on any given day? Collect data over a period of several days.*
>
> *How many students are likely to ask the teacher for a pencil on any given day?*
>
> *How many students are likely to be absent (or late) on any given day?*
>
> *How many scraps of paper are likely to be on the floor or in the waste basket at the end of any given day?*

Concept: <u>Construct sample spaces</u>

Using the creative drama lesson titled **Plot:Setting** on page 186, as a basis, ask the students to construct the setting to the scale of the space.

SCIENCE

Essential Element: The use of skills in acquiring data through the senses

Each grade has drama lessons in this book which focus on sensory awareness and sensory recall, which relate to this essential element in science.

Concept: <u>Observe that all living organisms depend on plants.</u>
See the lesson titled **Color**, page 168, for a direct application of this concept.

Concept: <u>Observe the cellular composition of organisms</u>
After observation, the students use movement and pantomime to demonstrate how the cellular composition works.

Concept: <u>Observe that energy can be changed from one form to another</u>
Energy changes can be demonstrated through movement and pantomime, with several students working together.

Essential Element: Experience in oral and written communication of data

Concept: <u>Describe changes in objects and events</u>
See the lesson titled **Fire**, on page 116, for a direct application of this concept.

Concept: <u>Describe animal behaviors</u>
     <u>Describe how plants and animals protect themselves</u>
Each student chooses one plant or animal to investigate. After the data has been collected, use an interview technique. The student becomes the plant or animal, and is interviewed by another student. The plant or animal reveals the appropriate behavior, while talking with the interviewer.

Essential Element: Experience in skills in relating objects and events to other objects and events

Concept: <u>Relate knowledge and skills of science to careers</u>

Each student chooses a particular career to find out about. The question is, "How has new technology changed that career?" Hold small panel discussions in which the students "become" the persons in that particular career, and discuss how their jobs have changed. Career possibilities are vast, of course. They may vary from musician to banker to doctor to pilot to homemaker. All are affected by the new technology.

HEALTH

The students can use a variety of dramatic methods to promote knowledge and understanding of good health practices: puppetry, masks, improvisations, mock interviews, preparing a videotape, writing and acting out a play. They may want to prepare a performance of some kind for a lower grade.

In each of the grades, the development of self-concept is noted as being an important essential element. Studies have found that participating in drama does promote a positive self-concept. The students learn that their ideas are valued and that they have a unique contribution to make. They each have the opportunity to be "in the spotlight" in a positive way.

PHYSICAL EDUCATION

Essential Elements:
Motor skills that develop positive body image and confidence. Rhythmic activities that develop coordination, self-expression, creativity, and endurance.

The rhythmic and interpretive movement lessons in this book relate very closely to the physical education elements. They will both extend and reinforce the physical education activities the children participate in.

226

Essential Element: Skills related to games and sports

Concept: <u>Develop and practice behavior reflective of good sportsmanship and safety</u>

Guide the students to construct hand puppets and create scenes which deal with sportsmanship. The children will be able to "hide" behind their puppets, and show how a good sport or a bad sport reacts and feels. They can use their voices to express the characters in a way they might feel self-conscious about without the puppet. Remind them that sometimes a person who wins a game behaves like a bad sport, as well as a person who loses.

The following titles may provide ideas for groups of children to create a short puppet scene:

> Manuel loses the race, but is cheered by all;
> Lisa wins the race, but loses friends;
> Everybody loses sometimes;
> "The referee (judge, umpire) has it in for me";
> "You tripped me on purpose";
> "Congratulations!"

FINE ARTS

ART

Many of the lessons in this book lend themselves to follow-up activities in art. Generally, after students have explored ideas through drama, they are much more aware of details than before. Drawings and paintings become more vivid and colorful. Students can also be guided to create an abstract design or painting which reflects the mood of what has been improvised in drama.

Essential Element: Inventive and imaginative expression through art materials and tools

Concept: <u>Express individual ideas, thoughts, and feelings in simple media</u>

1. Show the students pictures or, better yet, actual examples of sculpture.

Discuss the feelings evoked by the sculpture, as expressed by line and form. Discuss where sculptors get their ideas.

Divide the class into pairs. One becomes the sculptor, the other the piece of clay. The sculptor gently forms the clay into a sculpture expressing an idea, which is either realistic or abstract. Older students may want to express themes such as war, greed, love, joy and hope.

When the sculptures are completed, the class looks at them and reacts to the forms. Reverse the roles.

This can also be done with several people being the clay.

Some students may want to photograph the sculptures.

2. Students can be helped to understand the dynamics of line and form when they play out a series of "freeze-frame" movements. For example, two or more students are enacting a baseball play. One is the pitcher, another is up to bat. (Others can be the catcher, etc.) While they play, you periodically call out "freeze-frame." The players freeze their pose. Those who are watching discuss the line and form which communicates action.

Essential Element: Understanding and appreciation of self and others through art culture and heritage

Concept: <u>Look at and talk about contemporary and past artworks</u>

If at all possible, take the class to an art museum. If not, use slides or other art visuals.

1. Look at a painting, such as one of the Old West, and talk about the sensory elements communicated by the painting: the sights, the smells, the tastes, the various textures.

What sounds can be heard by viewing the painting? (For example, horses' hooves, guns, yelling, bodies falling.)

Divide the class into groups and orchestrate a "sound sculpture" to go with the painting. Each group is responsible for a certain sound effect. When you point to any given group, they make the sounds they have decided on. You can build this so that it starts out quietly, builds to a crescendo, and then recedes.

2. Look at a painting and discuss what is happening in the painting.
   What do you think happened just before the action in the painting?
   What might have happened afterward?
Divide them into groups. Some of the groups will create a tableau of the "before scene," some of the "after scene." Have two groups create their tableaus at once. If possible, the "before" group will position themselves on one side of the painting, the "after" group on the other side. The class responds by giving their perception of what they see happening in each tableau.

MUSIC

Essential Element: Singing concepts and skills

Concept: <u>Create dramatizations, movements, new words to songs</u>
   Songs can be used in much the same way stories are used as a basis for dramatization. The lessons on pantomime and improvisation can help prepare the students to dramatize songs. Consider not only dramatizing while the music is playing, but using the song as a basis for a more complete and extended dramatization. Some songs also lend themselves to playing one verse, acting that out, playing the second verse, acting, and so on.

Concept: <u>Perform contrasts including high/low, up/down, loud/soft,</u>
      <u>fast/slow, long/short, smooth/jerky</u>
   These contrasts can be reinforced by using body movements. For example, when higher notes are heard, the students move in the high level of space, when lower notes are heard, they move in the low level of space. Loud sound is accompanied by strong movements, soft sound by gentle movements.

Concept: <u>Recognize aurally the difference between repeated sections,</u>
      <u>contrasting sections, and sections that return after a contrast</u>

This concept can be effectively reinforced through movement. In groups, ask the students to create appropriate and very specific movements for a given section. Whenever that section of music is repeated, they repeat the movements. They can do the same for a contrasting section, selecting movements which are contrasting, as well.

Essential Element: Responses to music through moving and playing

Concept: <u>Move to express mood and meaning of the music</u>
The lessons on rhythmic movement and interpretive movement for each grade level relate to the music concept.

Concept: <u>Recognize visually letter names of notes on treble staff</u>
Students can become the notes on a staff, or on a keyboard. Whenever the C is read, for example, the person acting that note responds by a hand, or whole body, movement. Have them change the notes they act out, so they eventually have the chance to be (and recognize) every note.

SOCIAL STUDIES

Creative drama is an effective tool to teach many aspects of Social Studies because it helps the students internalize and understand the human interactions which underlie situations and events. People and events come "alive" for the students when they are acted out. Because the social studies content is so vast, the teacher must decide which specific subject holds the most dramatic possibilities and interest for the children. The most important aspect to explore is the feelings of the various people involved, and link those feelings to those the children have experienced. The following suggestions are only the tip of the iceberg.

Essential Element: Personal, social, and civic responsibilities

Concepts: <u>Support individuals' rights to have differing opinions</u>

Respect individuals' rights to hold different political and religious beliefs

Friends sometimes disagree about things, yet each one can be right. Discuss the following examples:

If you like baseball best and your friend likes football, who is right?

If one loves okra and the other hates it, who is right?

How could the person who hates okra react in a kind way to the one who loves it?

Ask the students to come up with examples in which their opinion is different from someone else's. In pairs, ask them to talk about a given topic in which each holds a different opinion. Then ask them to switch roles, so they are discussing it from the opposite viewpoint. The topics should be discussed on a peer to peer level, rather than child to parent. They can discuss topics as if they are both adults, if they wish.

One of the most wonderful things about living in the United States, of course, is that everyone has the right to hold different political and religious beliefs. Even though one person has a different belief from another, each should be respected.

How can you show respect for another person's convictions?

How can you discuss different beliefs, showing respect for one another?

Hold a panel discussion, with students who have different views about a topic which interests them. After each member of the panel talks about his or her beliefs, the class can join in the discussion. The point is to state one's views and listen and comment, showing respect for others.

Concept: Explain the role of compromise as a method of resolving conflicts

Ask the students to act out situations from their own lives in which the people eventually compromise in order to solve a problem. For example,

On a beautiful Saturday, one family member wants to go biking, another wants to go swimming, another wants to go to a movie.

Or, each wants to watch a different program on television.

Or, each wants to do something different over the winter holidays.

231

Ask the students to look in the newspapers for examples of how the leaders of nations have to use the method of compromise, too. They can hold a mini-United Nations, discussing a current issue.

Discuss the value of compromise.

Essential Element: Historical data about the United States and the world.

Concepts: <u>Identify causes of historical events or actions in United States history; identify contributions of various cultures, past and present, to world civilization;</u>
<u>Identify significant individuals and other contributions to history</u>

Individuals are generally recorded in history because of something important they did for the good of the people. They usually accomplished something after having overcome great obstacles and problems. The problems and the feelings of the people are the heart of drama. Choose situations to enact which show

how things were before a particular change,

how the people felt,

what happened to make the change,

and then how they felt after the change.

One such situation, for example, is the escape of slaves using the underground railroad.

What was the life of the slaves like?

What kinds of things did they do?

What would a typical day be like?

How did they feel about their lives?

Why did many of them want to escape?

Ask the class to imagine they are slaves. They wake up in the morning, knowing that this may be the day they are to make their escape, if they hear the signal to go.

How will they get their things together and keep their masters from suspecting what is going to happen?

How do they feel about leaving some of their family and friends?
How will they go about their work until they hear the signal?
How did the underground railroad work?
What dangers were involved?

They all play out the situation simultaneously. You can sidecoach them as they go through the escape, heightening the drama by introducing complications such as the following:

You hear footsteps behind you in the distance. Can you find a place to hide?
You smell smoke. What will you do?
At last you reach your destination. How do you feel?

History is filled with very powerful, dramatic events. For example, play out how the people felt just before and then during the seige of the Alamo. You do not have to have opposing sides. They can imagine the seige and act out what happened to the men involved. Some of the students could make sound effects of the battle. Again, it is important to discuss what might have been going through the minds of the people, and how they felt.

The Revolutionary War is also filled with dramatic possibilities, especially since George Washington's troops had such difficulties for a long period of time. What must that winter have been like at Valley Forge, when there was not enough food or clothing, when 3000 soldiers died? Yet by spring, those who were there had turned into a well trained army. How could that have happened?

Individuals from many different countries have made significant contributions to our culture. Games can be played in which important inventions are pantomimed, with the first team to name the inventor winning a point.

In a similar vein, various countries are noted for specific contributions. As a review, groups of children could be assigned a certain country. They are to act out the "gifts" or contributions made by that country. For example, contributions from ancient Greece include democracy, public discussion of ideas, jury trials, tragic and comic plays, sculpture, epic poetry, the Olympic games. Each of these contributions holds possibilities for pantomime.

Essential Element: Local, state, national and world geography.

Concept: <u>Know how landforms and climate interact</u>

Students can be greatly assisted in understanding the formation of mountains, plateaus, and so on, if they act out what happened physically. What causes eruptions, for instance, and what happens to the earth?

Concept: <u>Understand how people have adapted to and modified the physical environment</u>

Divide the students into groups, to depict how people lived — what they wore, what kind of housing they had, what they did, what they ate — that was directly influenced by where they lived and the climate. They may even want to use simple costumes, to give an idea of the people. Each group can enact a different region, to show the contrasts.

Essential Element: Psychological, sociological, and cultural factors affecting human behavior.

Concepts: <u>Describe how traditions, customs, folkways, and religious beliefs differ among individuals and groups</u>

<u>Identify holidays and celebrations in the nation that are cultural-group related</u>

<u>Identify the contributions of various cultures to the American way of life (art, literature, music, etc.)</u>

There may be no better way to understand other cultures than by dramatizing the culture, and especially their holidays which include music, art, dance, costume, and foods. It is especially effective if a child, parent or community member can come to the class and talk about the festivities, their origin, and why they are important today. If such a person is not available, there is a wealth of information in books.

234

OTHER LANGUAGES

When trying to communicate with someone who speaks a language we don't understand, pantomime is the time-honored method for "speaking." Pantomime is also an effective way to reinforce concepts and vocabulary when teaching another language. In fact, one of the concepts listed for learning other languages is that the student "recognize the role of nonlinguistic elements in communication." Just as body language is the base for learning English, it is also the base for learning other languages. Out of body language, pantomime, grows the need for speaking. There are many opportunities for using drama in teaching other languages. A few examples follow.

Essential Element: Speaking

Concepts: <u>Reproduce sounds and intonation patterns in meaningful contexts; use words, phrases, or sentences as appropriate; and use expressions needed for daily life situations</u>

1. In teams, one team pantomimes a word or phrase. The other team determines what it is and they repeat it in the language. The team which guesses correctly in the least amount of time wins.

2. One student plays a teacher, another plays a child. The teacher gives instructions to the child, in the language, and the child follows the instruction. For example, "Turn off the lights."

3. Each student is given a card with a word on it. There are duplicate cards for each word. A volunteer pantomimes his or her word — "table," for example. When the student who has the same word recognizes the pantomime, he or she stands up and says the word. The same can be done with phrases or sentences.

4. Pantomime the actions to songs and simple stories.

5. The students make sound effects at the appropriate time when you tell a story in the language. The example, the wind was blowing hard one nght. (The class makes the sound of wind.) A clap of thunder shook the house.

Continue with the story.

Essential Element: Reading

Concept: <u>Read familiar material with comprehension</u>
   If the children can read a story and then act out parts of it, you will know whether they comprehended the story or not.

Essential Element: Culture

Concept: <u>Experience various aspects of another culture</u>
   All cultures have special days of celebration. Planning and participating in a celebration is one of the most effective ways of learning about the culture. Food, costumes, music, dance, decorations — all lend themselves to understanding the culture, as well as learning vocabulary.

   You will find a number of helpful books in the library which tell of the customs and culture of specific lands. Two such books, for example, include a lot of information about Mexico: *Mexico is People, Land of Three Cultures,* by Barbara Nolen, published by Charles Scribner's Sons, 1973; and *Mexico, Giant of the South,* by Eileen Latell Smith, published by Dillon Press, 1983.

   You may also want to refer to the section on anthologies and collections, in Appendix B of this book. There are many stories from various cultures which give the flavor of the culture and are suitable for dramatization by the students.

Part Two
USING DRAMA WITH
SPECIAL POPULATIONS

Is a very real sense, all children, indeed all adults, are special. However, some children are set apart from what is considered "the norm," perhaps because of giftedness, learning disabilities, physical disabilities, emotional problems, or cultural differences. All of these children perceive themselves as "different," because society has cast them in that role. In fact, being children they are more "like" other children than they are "different." They all share some common needs: the need for acceptance, the need to communicate and express themselves, and the need for a positive self-concept. Experiences in the theatre arts address themselves to each of those needs in ways that provide great satisfaction to the child.

The Academically Gifted

Courses designed for the academically gifted are often rigorous and demanding, especially in the sciences and mathematics. Unfortunately, the social and creative aspects of development are frequently overlooked.

Even in the early grades, superior performance by gifted students is noticed by classmates, and unless the gifted child is also a social leader, he or she may not feel accepted by the other children. Through theatre arts activities, children can learn to work together and to respect one another.

Academically gifted children may or may not appear to be creative at first. But once the imagination is sparked, ideas will tumble out in rapid succession and even the most inhibited will find release in expression. These children are able to think of many things at once, understand structure, and perceive themes. They need a challenge and will be able to delve quite deeply into the material presented.

The Learning Disabled

Learning disabilities, of course, range from the fairly mild to the profound. The following suggestions are for those with mild learning disabilities — those children who are mainstreamed except for certain portions of the day — and those who are considered "educable mentally retarded."

1. Use coordination exercises, such as the rhythmic and imitative movement activities in this book. Coordination exercises are often prescribed for children with learning disabilities.

2. Help them learn through their kinesthetic, or muscle, sense. Activities in which they physically use their bodies to represent a concept, can be effective for retention of the concept:

    a. Draw large letters in the air.

    b. Walk the shape of a letter on the floor.

    c. Use the body to form the letter.

    d. Use the "Math Machine" activity on page 223.

    e. Act out words to reinforce their meaning and build vocabulary.

    f. Motivate the children to remember a story sequence by telling them they will be allowed to act out after they read it.

3. Give directions which are "uncluttered," direct and clear.

4. Praise and encourage over and over again.

5. Repeat the same activities often.

6. Set up "pretend" environments for the educable mentally retarded. Often the retarded child finds it difficult to use the imagination and relate to abstract ideas. Setting up a "restaurant" environment, for example, in one part of the room can be effective. Children show how one acts in a restaurant, looking at the menu, ordering, eating, and so on. They will enjoy pretending the food is really there — a leap in the imagination.

7. Key into the interests and needs of the children.

8. Provide a supportive and accepting environment. Helping the children develop self-confidence and a sense of self-worth is equally important as learning language and number concepts. They need experiences in which their contributions are valued and respected.

The Physically Disabled

Theatre arts activities are readily adaptable to children with various kinds of physical handicaps. Furthermore, such activities bring great joy to the participants, and satisfaction to the teacher who guides them. Perhaps the most important thing to remember is to choose activities in which the child will feel successful, and proud of making a worthwhile contribution. By believing in them, they are helped to believe in themselves. The following are a few suggestions for children with specific disabilities.

Hearing impaired children, whether they are partially hearing or totally deaf, can participate in many theatre arts activities.

1. Use the rhythmic movement, interpretive movement, and pantomime activities in the book.

2. Use a drum for rhythms, or a stick, like a broom handle, marking time on a wooden floor.

3. Select stories in which the plot can be communicated largely through pantomime.

4. In classes where children are "mainstreamed," consider having the hearing impaired children play the characters, signing and gesturing as the characters would, while hearing and speaking actors stand to the side and speak the dialogue at the appropriate time as the character would.

Partially sighted or blind children are generally comfortably with language.

1. Begin with imitative dialogue lessons.

2. Use rhythmic activities in a barrier-free space. One of the needs of this group is to become more comfortable with their own bodies and their relationship in space.

3. Begin movement activities which are confined to the area they are standing in, and then gradually increase the amount of space to move in. Moving freely in space is a special luxury that many will not have experienced before.

4. Encourage them to work in pairs, holding hands or touching in some way. Working with a partner may help them feel more secure.

5. Keep the setting constant for any given story. Blind children can dramatize stories, but the setting needs to be carefully delineated, so that a chair, for instance, is always in the same place. When they feel secure in the setting, they will be able to concentrate on the action and dialogue of the story.

Children with *limited movement capabilities* can also participate in drama.

1. Use rhythmic movements with any part of the body that can move: fingers, elbows, eyes, nose, mouth and so on.

2. "Dance" with a wheelchair! A mobile person manipulates the wheelchair in a rhythm.

3. Use puppets. They are particularly effective with those whose movement is limited. The puppet becomes the "alter ego" who can do everything the disabled person cannot do, and, in fact, the puppet can do things that no humans can do!

4. Adapt stories so they can accommodate a person in a wheelchair. For example, there isn't any reason that Tommy has to "skip down the road." He could "move down the road," or roll, or go, or amble along.

The Emotionally Unstable

The discussion here does not refer to severely emotionally disturbed individuals, but rather to those children with emotional problems who are still able to be in a regular classroom setting. The behavior of such children is often either very inhibited or very aggressive. Participation in drama activities can be very helpful, but using drama does not imply that the teacher should play "therapist." There are trained drama therapists for that. The teacher can guide drama activities, however, which may help inhibited children feel more confident to express themselves, and help aggressive children control their actions.

Inhibited or shy children often are lost in the classroom, because they do not cause any problems, nor do they demand attention. It is easy to become aware of them only when they are asked to respond verbally or to interact with others in some way. Classmates frequently "rescue" the child by saying, "He is shy, he won't talk," and then provide the answer for him. Such a child may have a very difficult time communicating ideas, which can be frustrating for the child, the teacher and the rest of the class. A great measure of patience and support is necessary.

The following are a few suggestions that may help shy children become involved. Once they allow themselves to become involved, they generally participate with no reluctance.

1. Begin each session with a movement warm-up that is exactly the same each time, or has only minor variations. This establishes a ritual which children respond to — they know what to expect.

2. Use rhythmic movement activities where everyone in the circle holds hands while moving.

3. Use rhythmic activities in which partners hold hands. You act as the partner for the inhibited child. Or, become the partner for two children, and during the activities have some excuse to move away and let the two children continue the movement, without you.

4. Ask the inhibited child to help you in small tasks, such as passing out something or turning on the lights.

5. Use puppets. Frequently, inhibited children learn to act freely when they can hide behind a puppet, or a mask.

6. Give gentle encouragement and positive reinforcement.

Very *aggressive* children present a different kind of challenge to the teacher. These children usually demand, and receive, attention for unacceptable classroom behavior. They need a lot of reinforcement for positive behavior. A few "hints" follow.

1. Plan many different activities, because these children usually have a short attention span.

2. Let them know that you want to have fun but you also mean business and will not put up with fights or playing around. If necessary, have them sit out for awhile, and permit them to return only so long as they obey the rules.

3. Use some activities in which individuals may volunteer to pantomime something for the group. Praise and applaud all volunteers. They need to feel better about themselves.

4. Always begin with a movement activity. As with inhibited children, aggressive children find security in ritual.

5. Ask the aggressive child to be your "assistant" sometimes.

6. Present a problem and ask the child for suggestions. For example, "We need to show that the crocodile is eating the monkey. How can we do this without touching? Susie, what do you think?" Then try out the idea offered by Susie, or use it to build upon.

7. Touch them occasionally on the back, or shoulder or arm, when they have done something well, or have tried to cooperate.

8. Speak calmly. If they misbehave, they pay the consequences by having to sit out. Speak to them matter-of-factly, and with sincere sympathy. For example, "Oh phooey, James, you forgot the rule. Sit over there for awhile. I'll bet you'll remember better next time." Then go right on with the rest of the group.

The Culturally Different and Economically Deprived

The term "culturally different" is *not* the same as "culturally deprived." All people belong to a culture, whether it is white, Hispanic, black, Asian, or something else. Each culture is rich in its heritage and values. Unfortunately, sometimes ethnic minorities are also economically deprived. Such children are like any other children, they just have a few special needs. A few suggestions follow:

1. Try to approach drama with these children from where they are in their daily lives. Many of them have never been exposed to anything but television and movies.

2. Start slowly, they will soon catch on to the idea of drama and delight in it.

3. Choose material that might seem slightly older than their actual age level. Many children from low income families are much more "street wise" than other children — they have had to fight for themselves. Don't ever talk down to them.

4. Choose stories with lots of action.

5. Don't let them shock you. Some will try with the things they say.

6. Keep abreast of the current trends and fads in music and clothes in whatever culture you are working with. Such awareness will help you understand the children, and, in turn, you will gain their respect.

7. Let them know that you want to have fun but you also mean business —you will not put up with fights or playing around. If necessary, call a halt to the drama if they behave in unacceptable ways. Ordinarily they are so hungry for a creative outlet that calling a halt will be enough to keep them quiet and behaving.

8. Give them as much caring attention as possible. Many get very little individual and personal attention in their daily lives.

It is common knowledge that no two snowflakes are alike. Upon close examination, one can see the unique qualities of each and appreciate the intricacy of the formations. In like manner, no two human beings are the same. Each one is special. When a child is looked at with close attention, one begins to appreciate the unique qualities of that human being. Teachers have the opportunity to bring out the specialness of each child, so that the child and others can recognize and appreciate the gifts each has to offer.

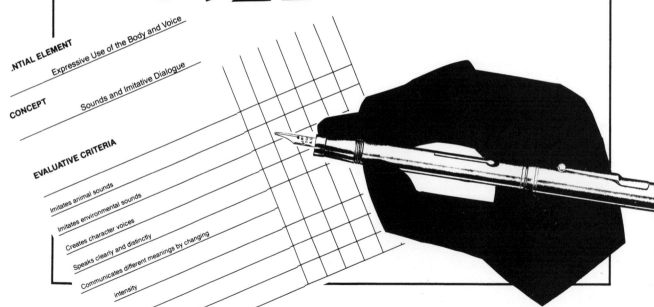

.NTIAL ELEMENT

Expressive Use of the Body and Voice

CONCEPT

Sounds and Imitative Dialogue

EVALUATIVE CRITERIA

Imitates animal sounds

Imitates environmental sounds

Creates character voices

Speaks clearly and distinctly

Communicates different meanings by changing

intensity

pitch

Chapter VI:
ASSESSMENT

Teachers employ evaluation strategies daily, making decisions that have a direct effect on the learning that is both possible and probable. In order to make valid judgments about what has been achieved both in teaching and in learning, there must be a clear understanding of objectives and the learning that is expected. Explicit evaluative criteria must be developed to ensure that evaluative decisions are educationally sound and communicate clearly to others.

In the theatre arts curriculum, evaluation should focus on individual growth as it is reflected in how the student participates in the creative process, what the student produces, and how the student responds to aesthetic experiences. Students should be measured against their own potential, recording where they start and how far they progress, rather than comparing students against each other.

There are basically two types of evaluation, "ongoing" and "summative." Ongoing evaluation helps teachers plan appropriate work for students, maximizing their strengths and identifying skills to be developed. Judgements about the student's work are employed directly, by talking about strengths and weaknesses, and indirectly, by structuring new experiences aimed at building upon previous achievements.

Summative evaluation documents the individual student's achievement at a specific time. Although ongoing evaluation is far more prevalent, summative evaluation is given more importance, causes more worry, and is thought of as "the real thing" by many students, parents, and administrators. Audiences for the two types of evaluation are normally different. Ongoing evaluation is employed in the everyday relationship between the student and teacher, whereas summative evaluation is used to inform parents about their child's progress and to determine promotion. It is, therefore, important for all concerned to know the precise purpose of any evaluation and to whom such information is directed.

EVALUATION STRATEGIES

There are a number of evaluation strategies which are appropriate to use in the theatre arts curriculum at the elementary level. They include class discussion, audio and videotape recording, problem solving projects, role playing, oral and written critiques, oral and written tests, and criteria checklists. Depending upon what is being evaluated, there are usually several options for assessment of any given objective.

Class discussion is one of the most commonly used strategies. In fact, teachers will note that class discussion is part of the creative drama process, called "evaluation," and is built into every lesson. The goal of such discussion is for students to learn how to evaluate their own and one another's work in a constructive manner. The discussion is based on questions from the teacher, some of which relate directly to the objective of the lesson.

Periodic use of **audio and videotape recordings** can help the students evaluate their own work more clearly, as well as help the teacher evaluate the students' progress. After two or three times, students will become accustomed to the camera and will behave as they normally do.

Problem solving projects require application of knowledge, critical choice, and decision making. Such activities are open-ended creative endeavors centering on the process rather than on preconceived products. Consequently, the teacher's personal values should not restrict student creativity. An example of such a project might be the following assignment: Develop a plot in which the conflict deals with people vs. the environment.

Role playing is related to problem solving projects. The student reveals understanding of a concept by applying it in action. For example, if the objective is to understand that a character's attitude often determines how he or she does something, the student might be assigned a certain character and a certain action, such as a mother baking cookies. The student then plays the role in several different ways: happy, because an old friend is coming to visit; irritated and rushed, because she was just informed she had to bring cookies to a meeting in an hour; tired and out of sorts, because she is coming down with a cold.

Aesthetic growth results from oral and written critiques of both student work and professional productions. **Oral critiques** by the students themselves can be started earlier in the grades than one might expect. The oral critiques grow out of class discussions where the tone is positive and constructive, rather than negative. Such critical analysis needs to be based on established critiera. Sometimes half the class may be pantomiming something, for example, and each person watching is assigned to focus on one particular person and comment on something specific, like what the person did to show he or she was walking through a thick forest, or a dark cave. **Written critiques** can be done in a similar manner, as the students develop writing skills.

Oral and written tests can be used to evaluate students' understanding of terminology and such concepts as plot structure, and character objectives. A written test might even take the form of writing a story with the intent to show clear plot structure, for example, or to describe the sequence of events in a story that was just acted out.

Criteria checklists can be very useful for evaluating individual student progress and achievement. Criteria focus on specific theatre arts objectives, as well as individual and group behaviors necessary for effective work in theatre arts. The same criteria for pre-assessment, ongoing, and summative evaluation can serve to document student progress toward mastery of stated objectives.

Whether the teacher chooses to use one method of assessment or several, notation of students' progress is important for planning future lessons. Since the teacher is actively involved with the students during a theatre arts class, observations will usually be recorded after a session. Periodic records, rather than daily notations are usually adequate, with the first and final sessions of a grading period being useful for revealing a continuum of progress toward mastery of the essential elements. Notations about every student may be made following one session, or the teacher may find it more manageable to evaluate different groups of students in different sessions. Observations may be all inclusive or limited to selected behaviors for different activities. (Use the

"NA" to indicate which behaviors are not being evaluated.)

The teacher may use a checklist format or a rating scale format. The simplest notation is the checklist, in which a check mark indicates desirable behavior has been observed, and a blank space indicates the need for improvement.

> | ✓ | = desirable behavior
> | | = needs improvement
> | NA | = not applicable

If a more detailed continuum of development is desired, a rating scale of 1-4 can be used, rather than a check/no check.

> | 1 | = poor
> | 2 | = fair
> | 3 | = good
> | 4 | = superior
> | NA | = not applicable

Teachers may choose to keep individual records for each student, or class records for specific lessons. Teachers may also want to consider asking the students to evaluate themselves periodically, using the same form as the teacher. Sample forms of the above follow, as well as suggested evaluative criteria for the three essential elements. The evaluative criteria forms may be used for an individual student, in which case the vertical bars would be lesson titles and dates; or the form may be used for the whole class, in which case vertical bars would be added and students' names written in. In the latter case, add the lesson title and date to the form. Teachers should feel free to adapt any of these forms to the needs of their particular classrooms.

DATE: _____   LESSON TITLE: _____

	S T U D E N T S													
ON-GOING DRAMA BEHAVIORS														
CONCENTRATION														
follows directions														
sustains involvement in activity														
IMAGINATION														
contributes original ideas														
reacts spontaneously														
solves problems creatively														
incorporates imaginative detail														
COOPERATIVE INTERACTION														
contributes to group effort														
listens courteously to others														
takes turns														
assumes role of leader														
assumes role of followers														
accepts group decisions														
NONVERBAL EXPRESSION														
uses appropriate gestures														
uses appropriate movement														
VERBAL EXPRESSION														
speaks clearly														
speaks expressively														
improvises dialogue														

continued

EVALUATION AND CRITICAL ANALYSIS

makes constructive contributions to discussion and evaluations													
incorporates improvements into playing													

ATTITUDE

cooperative, involved													
shy, inhibited													
disruptive, hostile													

STUDENT _____   PROJECT _____

CLASS/PERIOD_____   EVALUATOR_____ DATE_____

CRITERIA   −   +   COMMENTS

CRITERIA	Rating	COMMENTS
	1 2 3 4 NA	
	1 2 3 4 NA	
	1 2 3 4 NA	
	1 2 3 4 NA	
	1 2 3 4 NA	
	1 2 3 4 NA	
	1 2 3 4 NA	
	1 2 3 4 NA	
	1 2 3 4 NA	
	1 2 3 4 NA	
	1 2 3 4 NA	
	1 2 3 4 NA	
	1 2 3 4 NA	

1 = poor   2 = fair   3 = good   4 = superior   NA = not applicable

251

ESSENTIAL ELEMENT

Expressive Use of the Body and Voice

CONCEPT

Movement: Rhythmic and Imitative

EVALUATIVE CRITERIA

Repeats movements with precision							
Synchronizes movements							
Moves in various kinds of rhythms							
Moves body parts in isolation							
Creates contrasting movement patterns							
Moves easily in small and large spaces							
Knows a variety of locomotor movements							
Knows the difference between							
heavy and light movements							
Falls down safely							
Imitates the movements of a variety of animals							
Imitates the movements of a variety of							
inanimate objects							

252

ESSENTIAL ELEMENT

Expressive Use of the Body and Voice

CONCEPT

Sensory Awareness and Pantomime

EVALUATIVE CRITERIA

Responds appropriately to directions							
Describes sensory details of objects which are present							
Describes sensory details of objects which are not present							
Allows the senses to stimulate the imagination							
Clearly communicates animal movements							
Clearly communicates sensory properties of objects:							
size							
shape							
weight							
texture							
temperature							
Clearly communicates being in a specific place							
Clearly communicates specific activities							
Clearly communicates character movements and actions							

253

ESSENTIAL ELEMENT

Expressive Use of the Body and Voice

CONCEPT

Sounds and Imitative Dialogue

EVALUATIVE CRITERIA

Imitates animal sounds							
Imitates environmental sounds							
Creates character voices							
Speaks clearly and distinctly							
Communicates different meanings by changing							
intensity							
pitch							
volume							
rate of speed							

254

ESSENTIAL ELEMENT

Expressive Use of the Body and Voice

CONCEPT

Emotional Recall

EVALUATIVE CRITERIA

Evaluative Criteria									
Recalls and describes different feelings									
Uses body to express feelings									
Uses voice to express feelings									
Expresses appropriate feelings while acting out situations									
Expresses contrasting moods as a character other than self									

ESSENTIAL ELEMENT

Creative Drama

CONCEPT

Dramatize Literary Selections Using

Sensory Recall, Pantomime, Dialogue

EVALUATIVE CRITERIA

Sensory Recall							
Responds approximately to directions							
Describes sensory details of objects which are present							
Allows senses to stimulate the imagination							
Pantomime							
Clearly communicates animal movements							
Clearly communicates sensory properties of:							
size							
shape							
weight							
texture							
temperature							
Communicates being in a specific place							
Communicates specific activities							
Communicates character movements and actions							

256

continued

Dialogue

Creates character voices							
Speaks clearly and distinctly							
Communicates meaning by using vocal							
intensity							
pitch							
volume							
rate of speed							

Emotional Recall

Uses body to express feelings							
Uses voice to express feelings							
Expresses appropriate feelings while acting out situations							

Improvisation of Plot

Develops stories with clear beginning, middle, climax and ending							
Understands the three major sources of conflict							
Shows how the setting affects a plot							
Shows how time affects a plot							

continued

Characterization

Shows physical characteristics							
Shows characters' objectives							
Shows characters' attitudes							
Uses dialogue and voice to reveal character							
Listens and responds appropriately to others							
Sustains concentration / characterization							

Situation Role Playing

Enacts scenes from various points of view							
Sustains concentration							

258

ESSENTIAL ELEMENT

Creative Drama

CONCEPT

Dramatize Literary Selections Using

Puppetry and Shadow Play

EVALUATIVE CRITERIA

Constructs simple hand, body and shadow puppets						
Acts out the story or poem using						
appropriate movements for puppets						
character voices						
clear and distinct speech						
appropriate intensity						
appropriate pitch						
appropriate volume						
appropriate rate of speed						

ESSENTIAL ELEMENT

Aesthetic Growth Through Appreciation of Theatrical Events

CONCEPT

View Theatrical Events

EVALUATIVE CRITERIA

Player-Audience Relationship							
and Audience Etiquette							
Arrives promptly							
Talks quietly before performance							
Remains seated during performance							
Does not talk or eat during performance							
Responds attentively to performers							
Applauds at appropriate times							
Waits for turn to exit							
Characterization (Describes the following in relationship							
to the performance seen)							
physical characteristics							
objectives of characters							
how attitudes affected action							
actors' use of the voice							
actors' use of movement and pantomime							

260

continued

Plot

Describes the major conflict						
Describes how the setting affected the play						
Describes how the time affected the play						
Predicts plot resolution						
Suggests alternative courses of action						

Staging (Describes how the following contributed to the production.)

the set						
the lights						
the costumes						
the sound						
any special effects						

Evaluates and Makes Aesthetic Judgements

Discusses general response to theatrical event						
Gives reasons for comments, based on						
characterization						
plot						
staging effects						

ESSENTIAL ELEMENT

Aesthetic Growth Through Appreciation of Theatrical Events

CONCEPT

Recognize Similarities and Differences in

Television, Film and Live Theatre

EVALUATIVE CRITERIA

Describes similarities and differences with regard to

setting						
acting						
time of action						
special effects						
camera angles						
position of the audience						

262

THEATRE ARTS GLOSSARY OF TERMS

ACT — That part of the creative drama process in which the children portray characters in a scene or story.

AESTHETIC GROWTH — Increased understanding and appreciation of the art of drama.

CHARACTER — A person, animal, or entity in a scene, story, or play with distinguishing physical, mental, and attitudinal attributes.

CHILD DEVELOPMENT — Theatre arts help children develop awareness of themselves as physical beings, creative beings, social beings, organizers of experience, and active participants in their environment.

CHILDREN'S THEATRE — Plays presented for an audience of children.

CLOSING ACTIVITY — A quiet activity or discussion that is calming and helps prepare the children to participate in their next subject or activity with control.

COMMUNICATION — The process of interacting with another person or persons to give and receive messages, either verbally or nonverbally.

CONCENTRATION — The ability to focus and keep one's attention fixed on the matter at hand, to the exclusion of distracting factors.

CREATIVE DRAMA — "An improvisational, non-exhibitional, process-centered form of theatre in which participants are guided by a leader to imagine, enact, and reflect upon human experiences." (As defined by The Children's Theatre Association of America.)

DIALOGUE — The words used by the characters to communicate their thoughts.

DRAMA AS AN ART — Teaching in order to help children understand and appreciate the art of drama, which is a story told through action and dialogue.

DRAMA AS A TEACHING TOOL — Using drama as a teaching technique to enhance, extend, and deepen the understanding of concepts in other subject areas. Using drama in this way allows children to learn physically and kinesthetically, as well as mentally and emotionally. It helps total learning so that concepts are likely to be remembered.

EMOTIONAL AWARENESS — Activities to heighten awareness of feelings both in oneself and in others.

EMOTIONAL RECALL — The ability to remember feelings in order to recreate them with honesty and sincerity when playing a character.

EVALUATION — That part of the creative drama process in which personal efforts and efforts of others are reflected upon and appraised, after acting out a scene or story.

FANTASY — The use of imagination to create strange, unusual, or non-realistic characters or settings, such as creatures from outer space, or toys that talk.

GESTURE — An expressive movement that communicates an idea, a feeling, or state of being.

IMAGINATION — The process of forming a mental picture of what is not physically present or of what has not been personally experienced. Or, the process of combining images from previous experiences.

IMITATIVE DIALOGUE — Imitating the speech of stereotypical characters, such as a witch, a giant, a baby.

IMITATIVE MOVEMENT — Imitating the movement of characters, such as an elephant, a clown, a bird.

IMITATIVE SOUND — Imitating sounds, such as wind, thunder, animals.

IMPROVISATION — The spontaneous creation of a character through action and speech, in a particular situation.

INTERPRETIVE MOVEMENT — Movement used to depict non-human roles or abstract concepts.
Examples: fire, wind, power, love

INTRODUCE — That part of the creative drama process in which the teacher presents a motivating activity or discussion, preparing the children for the activity or story to follow and helping them to identify with a given character or situation. An effective introduction stimulates the children's thoughts and their feelings.

MOVEMENT — Activities which focus on the body using variations of time, space and energy to communicate ideas or feelings.

ORIGINAL DIALOGUE — Improvising the dialogue for a character.

PANTOMIME — Action, movement and gesture, without words.

PERCEPTION — The process by which people use their senses to gain information from the physical environment. It may be as simple as identifying the color of a fabric or the tone of a sound, or as complex as describing a plot line or creating a character.

PLAN — That part of the creative drama process in which the teacher asks questions to help children understand the action and feelings of the characters and the sequence of the plot, in preparation for acting it out.

PLAYING — Improvising or acting-out characters in a scene or story.

PLAYING IN ROLE — A technique used by the leader during the playing, or acting, in which the leader plays a role that allows for some authority and control, to heighten and advance the playing.

PLOT — The story revealed through the action and dialogue of the characters. Plot structure usually includes a beginning, middle, and end; it has a problem, complications, climax and resolution.

PUPPETRY — The animation of objects to create characters in dramatic situations.

QUESTIONS — Open-ended questions that begin with why, what, when, where, how, and who, encourage discussion. Closed questions that elicit yes-or-no responses discourage discussion. Examples: How did the character show her power? (open-ended) Did the character show her power? (closed)

REACTION — Responding to a stimulus. Drama is built upon the action and reaction of the characters.

REPLAYING — Enacting the scene or play again, making improvements, and sometimes changing roles so that the children have the opportunity to play more than one character.

RHYTHMIC MOVEMENT — Activities that have a certain rhythmic pattern.

ROLE PLAYING — Enacting a role (character) other than oneself in an improvisation based on a given dramatic situation.

SENSORY AWARENESS — Experiences to sharpen perception and open senses to heightened awareness.

SENSORY RECALL — The ability to remember sensory experiences in order to recreate them accurately.

SHADOW PLAY — A form of puppetry using flat puppets, hands, or human silhouettes presented behind a backlighted sheet.

SIDECOACHING — A technique using by the leader during the playing, or acting, in which the leader offers suggestions or comments from the side of the playing area, to heighten and advance the playing.

SITUATION ROLE PLAYING — Improvisations which focus on understanding the viewpoints of others.

SPATIAL PERCEPTION — Activities which focus on how the body moves in space and how characters move in relationship to one another.

SPECTACLE — The external staging devices, such as sets, props, lights, and costumes, used to enhance and clarify the plot and characters.

STORY DRAMATIZATION — Improvising a story based on literature.

THEME — The main thought of the improvisation or play, developed through the plot and characters.

WARM-UP — An activity in which the children focus their attention on limbering up their bodies and/or voices.

Appendices

Appendix A

IDEA STARTERS

These activities can be used as jumping off places for your own ideas for dramatization. Or they can be used, as written, for those one to five minute interludes which often occur during a day, or when the children need an action-break from other classroom work. The suggestions are not placed in any sequential order. Use those which seem appropriate for your class situation.

HOLIDAYS AND SEASONS

A. Halloween

1. Build a dramatization around the witches' chant, from Act IV, Scene 1, of *Macbeth,* by William Shakespeare:

> Double, double toil and trouble,
> Fire burn and caldron bubble.
>
> Fillet of a fenny snake,
> In the caldron boil and bake.
> Eye of newt and toe of frog,
> Wool of bat and tongue of dog,
> Adder's fork and blindworm's sting,
> Lizard's leg and howlet's wing,
> For a charm of powerful trouble,
> Like a Hell broth boil and bubble.
>
> Double, double toil and trouble,
> Fire burn and caldron bubble.

2. Ask students to imagine that it is midnight on Halloween. They are in their beds, sleeping, when they feel a spell being cast on them. They feel very strange. In slow motion they change into something else. Instead of being evil, however, they find they are a powerful force for good. They are given one hour to accomplish the thing that would be most helpful to the world.

B. Thanksgiving

1. Ask each student to think of one thing he or she could do that a particular family member would be thankful for. They pantomime the activities.

2. In small groups, students act out a scene evolving around something they are thankful for.

C. Winter Holidays

1. Brainstorm ideas about how the winter holidays could be happier for people less fortunate than they are. For example, people in old folks homes, people without homes, children in hospitals. In groups, students act out what they might do to make the holidays happier for a particular group of people. Later, they may even decide to follow through in reality!

2. Students take turns pantomiming their favorite activity of the winter holidays.

D. Fall

1. They pantomime activities that take place in the Fall. Football, for example, is more than just the game. There are marching bands, drill teams, twirlers, people selling food and programs, to name a few.

2. Fall signals the start of a new school year. Students act out one of their favorite things about school. If you are willing, they can even act out their least favorite thing!

E. Winter

1. The pantomime something they like to do best in the winter.
2. Dramatize the Greek myth of Demeter and Persephone.
3. Act out what they like least about winter.

F. Spring

1. They pantomime games they like to play outside in nice weather.
2. They pantomime flying a kite on a windy day. What happens when it gets caught in a tree?
3. Each one pretends to *be* the kite.

G. Summer

1. What are some activities they are looking forward to doing in the summer? They show their ideas, rather than telling.

2. They go exploring in the woods and come upon something very mysterious. What is it and what will they do?

3. They are bored; there doesn't seem to be anything to do. Suddenly they look up and see a strange light flashing all over the room. Whatever the light is, it wants to take them on an adventure. What will the adventure be? How will they get there?

H. Birthdays

1. They think of a present that begins with the first initial of the birthday person's first or last name, or the month in which he or she was born. They pantomime the presents. For example, Manuel Garcia might get a motorcycle, a mouse, a mermaid, a gorilla, a glove, a garbage disposal. This activity can be done individually, or in groups.

SENSES

A. Touch (They should keep their eyes closed to help focus on the tactile sense.)

1. Students touch various parts of their chairs and describe the way it feels.

2. In pairs, they find something for their partner to touch. the partner describes it and tries to identify it.

3. They touch selected objects with various textures, and tell what other things have a similar texture to what they are touching.

4. In pairs, they explore their partners hands by touch. Then eight or ten students form a circle. One person is in the middle and, with eyes closed, tries locate his or her partner by touching the hands of the people in the circle.

B. See

1. Play "Twenty Questions," with something clearly visible in the room. One person decides what the object is. The others ask questions about it that can be answered "Yes," or "No." They must be able to identify the object by the time twenty questions are asked.

2. After looking at a picture for thirty seconds, they write a list of all the things they remember about the picture. Compare lists.

3. Crumple a plastic garment bag, such as you get from the cleaners, into a small ball. Then open your hands. While the plastic changes form, students tell the various things it reminds them of.

4. With eyes closed, students "see" an alligator walking down the street toward them. Give them one minute to use their inner vision to see what happens. Talk about it.

C. Hear (eyes closed)

1. Make some sounds, such as adjusting a window blind, turning pages in a book, pouring water in a glass. Ask students to identify the sounds, in the order in which they heard them.

2. In pairs, students make a series of sounds for their partners to identify in sequence. They begin with three sounds, then keep increasing the number of sounds until they can't remember them in sequence.

3. Ask students to recall a family member's voice. How does it sound when the person is excited, when he or she is angry? They describe the voices.

4. They listen to a piece of music and raise their hands when they hear either a certain instrument, a particular melody, when the drum came in, and so on.

D. Taste

1. They pantomime eating their favorite food, noticing how it feels in their mouth. They describe the way it feels and tastes.

2. They think of something with a hot temperature and pantomime eating it. Then they think of something that is "hot," such as a jalapeno pepper, and imagine they are eating that. What are the differences? Does the hot sensation occur at difference places in the mouth in the two different experiences?

3. They imagine they are eating something very cold. Describe the taste and feel of the food.

E. Smell

1. They think of their favorite smell and the environment in which they smell it. As they imagine the environment, they will recall the smell.

2. Discuss smells that are peculiar to certain places or situations. Examples might include the woods after a heavy rain, outside on a hot summer day, freshly cut grass, a room with people smoking, the ocean.

ADVENTURES

1. They go on a rescue mission. Where? In space, under water, in a cave, in a burning house, on a lake, in the mountains, in the woods, at a circus, in the desert, in a grocery store, on an airplane?

2. They are explorers. What are they looking for? Treasure, secrets to a lost city, the secret to eternal youth, the cure for certain diseases, the key to world peace?

3. They turn back the clock of time, or turn it forward, to discover what it was like (or will be like) in other times and other places. They can use this chant while rotating all together in a large circle, with arms on each others' shoulders. They move either clockwise or counter clockwise, depending on whether they are going forward or back in time:

> Time, time, go away,
> We want another place,
> We want another day.

Repeat the chant three times, increasing the volume each time. Where will they go? Who will they be? What will they do? Will they journey to prehistoric times, revolutionary times, the Old West, Hiroshima, the United States in a thousand years, a new planet?

PROBLEM SOLVING

(You describe the situation, the students either respond immediately, or they can work in groups to act out the situation.)

1. What would you do if you came home and discovered your house had been burglarized?
2. What would you do if you were new in school, and no one would play with you?
3. What would you do if a fire started while you were babysitting at a neighbor's house?
4. What would you do if there were no schools to attend?
5. What would you do if it was the holiday season and your family had no money for presents?
6. What would you do if you got lost in the woods, just as night was beginning to fall?
7. What would you do if your pet suddenly started talking to you in your own language?
8. What would you do if you were told you could have three wishes?
9. What would you do if you had to make dinner for your favorite television actor? What food would you prepare? Who else would you invite? What would you talk about?
10. What would you do if, suddenly, your best friend wouldn't speak to you?

RELAXATION

(The following are images which can aid relaxation. Students may have others to add.)

1. The sound and sight of waves rolling up on the beach.
2. Being in a boat, alone, on a nice, calm day.
3. Being a lump of clay that someone is shaping lovingly and carefully.
4. Floating on a cloud.
5. Lying in the sun, with a gentle breeze blowing.
6. Listening to your favorite music.
7. Standing on a mountain top, surveying the world.
8. Watching a bright light that slowly gets dimmer and dimmer.
9. Sitting by a stream, watching the sun play on the water and small fish swimming about.
10. Being a lazy cat, sleeping in the sun, on a hammock gently rocked by a breeze.

CHILDREN'S LITERATURE: AN ANNOTATED BIBLIOGRAPHY

Anthologies and Collections

Anderson, Bernice G. *Trickster Tales from Prairie Lodgefires*
Nashville, TN: Abingdon, 1979.
Tales from Blackfoot, Kiowa, Crow, Ponca, Dakota and Cheyenne tribes.

Appich, Peggy. *Tales of an Ashanti Father*. New York: Dutton, 1981.
Anansi stories and "how and why tales" from West Africa.

Brown, Dee. *Teepee Tales of the American Indian*. New York: Holt,
Rinehart & Winston, 1979.
Tales, from a variety of Indian tribes, which are set in times when animals lived as equals with people.

Buck, Pearl. *Fairy Tales of the Orient*. New York: Simon and Schuster, 1965.
Many tales worthy of dramatizing from China, Japan, India, Turkey, Russia, Persia, Arabia and Egypt.

Dobie, J. Frank. *Tales of Old-Time Texas*. Boston: Little, Brown and Company, 1955.
Includes tales about well known characters, such as Jim Bowie, Sam Bass, Sam Houston, as well as tales about animals.

Dolch, Edward W. and Marguerite P. Dolch. *Stories from Japan*. Champaign, Illinois:
Garrard Publishing Company, 1960.
Folk tales rich with potential for dramatizing. Many favorites are included, such as "Momotaro, the Peach Boy," "Little One-Inch," and "Urashimo."

Fitzgerald, Burdett. *World Tales for Creative Dramatics and Storytelling*.
Englewood Cliffs, NJ: Prentice-Hall, 1962.
A fine collection of less well-known stories, grouped geographically, with cross-referenced recommendations according to age groups.

Green, Lila. *Tales from Hispanic Lands*. Morristown, NJ: Silver Burdett, 1979.
Nine tales from Spain, South America, Mexico and Puerto Rico.

Hall, Robin. *Three Tales from Japan*. New Orleans: Anchorage Press, 1973.
The dramatized folk tales include "The Magic Fan," "The Princess of the Sea," and "Little Peach Boy." Although intended to be produced by adults for children, older children would enjoy the challenge of acting them out themselves.

Jagendorf, Mortiz. *Folk Stories of the South*. New York: Vanguard Press, 1972.
A compilation of Indian myths, ghost stories, strongman tales, border episodes, and noodletales.

Jagendorf, Mortiz and Virginia Weng. *The Magic Boat and Other Chinese Folk Stories*.
New York: The Vanguard Press, 1980.
Folk tales from the People's Republic of China, reflecting the land's many minorities and the cultural history of the people.

Kipling, Rudyard. *Just So Stories*. New York: Shocken Books, 1965.
These wonderful "why" stories are excellent for dramatizing and also for stimulating the children to develop their own "why" stories.

Lester, Julius. *Knee-high Man and Other Tales*. New York: Dial, 1972.
Six delightful animal stories from Black folklore.

Lindsey, David L. *The Wonderful Chirrionera and Other Tales from Mexican Folklore*.
Austin, Texas: Heidelberg Publishing, Inc., 1974.
Droll stories with imaginative endings, accompanied by striking woodcuts by Barbara Mathews Whitehead.

Lyons, Grant. *Tales the People Tell in Mexico*. New York: Julian Messner, 1972.
Includes delightful tales, as well as a glossary and a section detailing the background of the stories.

Mar, S. Y. Lu. *Chinese Tales of Folklore*. New York: Criterion Books, 1964.
A collection of ancient Chinese stories. Historical notes precede each story, relating each tale to a definite period and real people of the past.

Ritchie, Alice. *The Treasure of Li-Po*. New York: Harcourt, Brace and World, Inc. 1949.
Six stories which capture the humor and dignity of the Chinese people.

Sheehan, Ethna. Folk and Fairy Tales from Around the World. New York:
Dodd, Mead and Company, 1970.
Stories from many countries, including Spain, Brazil, East Africa, India, Japan, China.

Siks, Geraldine B. *Children's Literature for Dramatization: An Anthology*.
New York: Harper & Row, 1964.
A leading authority in the field has collected and written poems and stories which are especially good for dramatizing. She makes suggestions about their use in creative drama classes.

Ward, Winifred. *Stories to Dramatize*. New Orleans: Anchorage Press, 1986.
This book first appeared in 1952 and has been a favorite with teachers since that time. Stories and poems are grouped according to age levels.

Wyndham, Robert. *Tales the People Tell in China*. New York: Julian Messner, 1971.
Classic illustrations grace this book of stories based on old tales, but written for contemporary children. The tales reflect all levels of Chinese society, customs and religion.

Books for Intermediate Grades

Some of the plots in these stories may be too complex to act out in their entirety. There are, however, many scenes from the stories which can be singled out for dramatizing.

Aiken, Joan. *Far Forests*. New York: Viking, 1977.
Mysterious and fantastic characters people these tales of romance, fantasy and suspense.

Andersen, Hans Christian. *Dulac's Snow Queen, and Other Stories from Hans Andersen*.
New York: Doubleday, 1976.
A beautifully illustrated book of the famous Andersen tales. Children can easily empathize with many of the characters in these stories.

Beachcroft, Nina. *Wishing People*. New York, Dutton, 1982.
Martha received a wonderful present on her tenth birthday — a weather house she had been pining for. She is amazed and delighted when the figures come to life and give her ten wishes. She finds out, however, that wishes can be very tricky.

Bodelsen, Anders. *Operation Cobra*. New York: Lodestar, 1979.
An exciting tale, set in Copenhagen. Frederik discovers his family is being held hostage by three terrorists. Frederik and his friends cleverly solve the problem.

Bradbury, Ray. *Halloween Tree*. New York: Knopf, 1972.
Trick-or-treaters encounter Carapace Clavicle Moundshroud who explains the origin of Halloween by taking them on a fantastic journey. At the end, he asks "which was it — trick or treat?" There is no hesitation — "Both."

Brittain, Bill. *Wish Giver*. New York: Harper & Row, 1983.
A delightfully funny and suspensful story. The characters' wishes do come true, but not as they had intended. There is a play on figurative versus literal language.

Budbill, David. *Snowshoe Treck to Otter River*. New York: Dial, 1976.
Three short stories about two boys who camp in the wilderness. Adventures include an encounter with wild creatures, falling into an icy river, and building a lean-to camp.

De Paola, Tomie. *Legend of the Bluebonnet*. New York: Putnam, 1983.
A favorite Texas tale, beautifully illustrated, in which a small orphan girl saves the land from drought.

Harding, Lee. *Fallen Spaceman*. New York: Harper Row, 1980.
An exciting science fiction story. A human-like alien crashes through space onto Earth. Two boys see the fall and go to investigate. One of the boys slips into what seems to be a huge space suit and it takes off into the forest.

Hooks, William H. *Mean Jake and the Devils*. New York: Dial, 1981
Three stories derived from the Jack Tales of North Carolina. Good Halloween stories.

Jacob, Helen Pierce. *Diary of the Strawbridge Place*. New York: Atheneum, 1978.
The Strawbridge place was an underground railway stop operated by a Quaker family. This is an exciting tale with many episodes, including a hunt to round up slaves who escaped from Kentucky. Dire circumstances prevail.

Krensky, Stephen. *Castles in the Air and Other Tales*. New York: Atheneum, 1979.
Five stories are plotted around a phrase or cliche: Castles in the Air; A Fine Kettle of Fish; The Last Straw; Too Clever for Words; A Barrel of Fun. The stories are good motivators for children to design their own stories and act them out.

Lane, Rose Wilder. *Young Pioneers*. New York: McGraw-Hill, 1961.
The trials of pioneer life are depicted. The characters face grasshoppers devouring their crops, blizzards, lonliness and attacking wolves.

L'Engle, Madeleine. *Wrinkle in Time*. New York: Farrar, Straus & Giroux, 1962.
Meg and friends are taken to another world by three extraterrestrial beings. They find Meg's father, but undergo many trials before they can free him from captivity.

Lobel, Arnold. *Fables*. New York: Harper & Row, 1980.
These are modern fables in which the animals are in ridiculous situations. For example, "The Crocodile in the Bedroom." A good book for stimulating children to think up their own fables.

Mendoza, George. *Gwot! Horribly Funny Hairticklers*. New York: Harper & Row, 1967.
Three scary stories from American folklore. The reader, or listener, has to decide what happens at the climax of each story. Groups of children can dramatize their ideas of the climax.

Montgomery, R. A. *A Journey Under the Sea*. New York: Bantam, 1979.
In these stories, the reader becomes the main character and determines how the plot evolves. Excellent for dramatizing and learning about plot.

Norton, Mary. *Borrowers Avenged.* San Diego, CA: Harcourt Brace Jovanovich, 1983.
  Another in the series of books about the Clock family who are tiny people, no taller than a pencil. They escape from a wicked couple and find an old rectory to live in.

Slote, Alfred. *My Robot Buddy.* Philadelphia, PA: Lippincott, 1975.
  This story takes place in the future — where robots are common-place. Some robots act as companions for children. Danny gets such a robot for his tenth birthday — and the excitement commences.

Walsh, Jill Paton. *Green Book.* New York: Farrar, Straus & Giroux, 1982.
  A good science fiction book about a group of colonists who are fleeing the dying Earth. They go to a new planet. The children are able to cope better than the adults, and they discover the secrets to survival.

Appendix C

ADDITIONAL RESOURCES

Creative Drama

Cottrell, June. *Teaching with Creative Dramatics*. Skokie, IL.: National Textbook, 1975.
   Teachers of young children will find this methods book extremely useful, extending dramatic play to sensory and movement experiences and culminating in creative drama.

Ehrlich, Harriety W., ed. *Creative Dramatics Handbook*. Urbana, IL.: National Council of Teachers of English, 1974.
   This book is made up of a series of practical lesson plans written by Philadelphia teachers. Many of the lessons use creative drama to teach other subjects, such as language arts, mathematics, and Afro-American history.

Furness, Pauline. *Role-Play in the Elementary School: A Handbook for Teachers*. New York: Hart Publisher, 1976.
   Fifty role-play lesson plans are presented which could be helpful in everyday classroom situations.

Goodridge, Jane. *Creative Drama and Improvised Movement for Children*. Boston: Plays, Inc., 1970.
   Many specific lesson ideas are presented, as well as helpful suggestions about evaluation of class progress.

Heinig, Ruth. *Creative Drama for the Classroom Teacher*. Englewood Cliffs, NJ: Prentice-Hall, 1981.
   Pantomime, improvisation, songs, stories, and games are arranged to demonstrate simple to complex techniques.

McCaslin, Nellie. *Creative Drama in the Classroom*. (4th ed.) New York: Longman, Inc., 1984.
   This is a comprehensive book which covers almost all aspects of drama with children. The teacher will find many useful activities.

McIntyre, Barbara. *Creative Drama in the Elementary School*. Itasca, IL.: F.E. Peacock, 1974.
   Specific classroom suggestions are given for primary and upper elementary teachers.

Pierini, Mary Paul Frances. *Creative Dramatics: A Guide for Educators.*
New York: Herder and Herder, 1971.
This is a resource book with verbal and visual ideas to stimulate drama in the classroom.

Polsky, Milton. *Let's Improvise.* Englewood Cliffs, NJ.: Prentice-Hall, 1980.
Ideas are presented for people of all age levels and for all levels of experience.

Schwartz, Dorothy, and Dorothy Aldrich, eds. *Give Them Roots . . . And Wings!*
Revised edition. New Orleans: Anchorage Press, 1985.
Lessons specifically designed for teachers, with goals, activities, and evaluation suggestions.

Siks, Geraldine Brain. *Drama with Children.* 2nd ed. New York: Harper
& Row, Inc., 1983.
This is a book for those who are interested in the theoretical basis behind child drama, as
well as activities which illustrate the theory.

Stewig, John Warren. *Informal Drama in the Elementary Language Arts Program.*
New York: Teachers College Press, 1983.
Specific ways are given in which movement and improvisation assist in the development of
language skills.

Stewig, John Warren. *Spontaneous Drama: A Language Art.*
Columbus: Merrill, 1973.
Drama is used to motivate reading, oral language development, nonverbal communication,
vocabulary development, and listening skills.

Valeri, Michele, and George Meade. *Have You Roared Today? A Creative Drama
Handbook.* Rockville, MD.: Montgomery County Public Schools, 1979.
Specific classroom activities are listed according to grade, materials needed, procedures, and
suggestions for sidecoaching.

Wagner, Betty Jane. *Dorothy Heathcote: Drama as a Learning Medium.*
Washington, D.C.: National Education Association, 1976.
The author carefully describes the methods used by Heathcote, a reknown British drama
teacher. Her special techniques include playing in role, questioning, and time for reflection.

Way, Brian. *Development Through Drama.* New York: Humanities Press, 1972.
This book contains capsulized, practical ideas for all teachers, as well as a philosophical basis
for using drama for child development.

Wilder, Rosilyn. *A Space Where Anything Can Happen: Creative Drama in a
Middle School.* Rowayton, CT.: New Plays Books, 1977.
The author has written an inspiring, yet practical, methods book. Clear guidelines are given
for helping contemporary children do creative work.

Puppetry

Boylan, Eleanor. *Puppet Plays for Special Days*. Rowayton, CT: New Plays, Inc. 1976.
This book provides a collection of short plays that should be welcomed by the classroom teacher who is looking for puppet material.

Brooks, Courtaney. *Plays and Puppets Etcetera*. Claremont. CA: Belnice Books, 1981.
This is a charming book written for those with little or no experience with puppetry.

Engler, Larry, and Carol Fijan. *Making Puppets Come Alive*. New York: Taplinger, 1973.
This book not only offers help in making and handling puppets, it also provides assistance about how to put on the puppet show.

Freericks, Mary, and Joyce Segal. *Creative Puppets in the Classroom*. Rowayton, CT: New Plays, Inc., 1979.
The authors show how puppets can be integrated into the curriculum. Simple techniques and inexpensive materials are encouraged.

Hunt, Tamara, and Nancy Renfro. *Puppetry in Early Childhood Education*.
Austin, TX. Nancy Renfro Studios, 1982.
This books deals with all aspects of puppetry. Teachers will find it extremely helpful.

Renfro, Nancy. *Puppetry and the Art of Story Creation*. Austin, TX: Nancy Renfro Studios, 1979.
The book stresses how to create stories with the children, using simple puppets. A section of the book deals with using puppetry with disabled individuals.

Schmidt, Hans J., and Karl J. Schmidt. *Learning with Puppets*. Chicago: Coach House Press, 1980.
This book focuses on using puppetry to help teach academic and social skills.

Sims, Judy. *Puppets for Dreaming and Scheming*. Walnut Creek, CA: Early Stages, 1978.
This book has a wealth of ideas, with clear directions, especially suited for teachers of younger children.

Special Populations

Behrn, Snyder, and Clopton. *Drama Integrates Basic Skills: Lesson Plans for the Learning Disabled.* Springfield, IL: Charles C. Thomas, 1979.
A practical text demonstrates ways a drama curriculum can help children integrate basic affective and cognitive skills.

Champlin, John, and Connie Brooks. *Puppets and the Mentally Retarded Student.* Austin, TX: Nancy Renfro Studios, 1980.
This book focuses on developing literary comprehension with the mentally retarded child. Special techniques are described for using puppets in elementary classrooms.

Gillies, Emily P. *Creative Dramatics for All Children.* Washington, D.C.: Association for Childhood International, 1973.
A well qualified teacher discusses drama for the emotionally disturbed and physically handicapped child, as well as those who speak English as a second language.

Jennings, Sue. *Remedial Drama: A Handbook for Teachers and Therapists.* New York: Theatre Art Books, 1978.
The author has presented a concise, easy to read, book about the values of drama for special populations.

McIntyre, Barbara. *Informal Dramatics: A Language Arts Activity for the Special Child.* Pittsburgh: Stanwix, 1963.
This book is a practical guide for teachers of special education.

Shaw, Ann M., and Cj Stevens. *Drama, Theatre and the Handicapped.* Washington, D.C.: American Theatre Association, 1979.
A collection of essays by prominent practitioners in the field provides descriptions of the kinds of programs available which encourage participation by handicapped people.

Shaw, Ann M., Wendy Perks and Cj Stevens, eds. *Perspective: A Handbook in Drama and Theatre by, with and for Handicapped Individuals.* Washington, D.C.: American Theatre Association, 1981.
A practical collection of activities and resources are presented, representing all aspects of handicapping conditions.

Wethered, Audrey G. *Drama and Movement in Therapy.* London: MacDonald and Evans, 1980.
This book is a practical guide to the therapeutic use of movement, mime, and drama.

Music

The *right* musical accompaniment for a drama lesson can stimulate (or calm) the children, create a mood and heighten the action. Music should be selected with great care. If you cannot find music that seems just right to you, it is better not to use it at all. Be prepared to listen to a lot of music.

The following list is like a "starter" — they are pieces which create certain moods. A number of them have several possibilities on a given album. You will discover your own preferred collection as you listen and imagine the action possibilities.

You will note that the pieces listed are mostly classical, and certainly without words. One wouldn't use a piece of music with words unless the words were a part of what was being acted out. You can use popular music, as long as it suits the action. Just remember that popular music will remind the children of a lot of things that may not be a part of the focus for the intended dramatization.

Bartok, *Music for Strings, Percussion and Celesta.*
Circus Time, Music Corporation of America Records, Ringling Brothers and Barnum & Bailey Circus Band, Merle Evans, conductor.
Debussy, *Afternoon of a Faun.*
Dukas, *Sorcerer's Apprentice.*
Grieg, *Peer Gynt Suite,* No. 1, "In the Hall of the Mountain King," "Morning"
Grofe, *Grand Canyon Suite,* "Cloudburst," "Sunrise."
Holst, *The Planets Suite.*
Kabalevsky, *The Comedians,* "March and Comedians' Gallop," "Pantomime."
Moussorgsky, *Pictures at an Exhibition.*
Ravel, *Daphnis and Chloe,* "Daybreak"
Saint-Saens, *Danse Macabre.*
Stravinsky, *The Firebird Suite.*
Tchaikowsky, *The Nutcracker Suite.*
Varese, *Poem Electronique.*
Varese, *Integrales.*

INDEX

BIOGRAPHY

Barbara T. Salisbury is a professor of drama at The University of Texas at Austin, where she works primarily in the area of creative drama. She received her Ph.D in curriculum and instruction and her undergraduate and master's degrees in theatre from the University of Washington. Salisbury has served as senior consultant for the television series, *Arts Alive!,* editor of the children's magazine, *Artsploration,* and co-author of several volumes on drama for children. She has earned recognition from her peers by being elected President of both the Children's Theatre Association of America, and the American Association of Theatre for Youth, and by receiving the Creative Drama for Human Awareness Award.